Understanding Monogamy

Belinda Tobin

UP

UNDERSTANDING PRESS

Understanding Monogamy

Copyright © 2024 by Belinda Tobin

Published by Understanding Press

UP

Paperback ISBN: 978-1-7637062-6-2

E-Book ISBN: 978-1-7637062-7-9

For permissions or enquiries, please contact:

Understanding Press

Email: up@heart-led.pub

Website: www.heart-led.pub/understanding-press

First Edition: October 2024

A catalogue record for this book is available from the National Library of Australia

Other titles in The Understanding Series:

Understanding Violence

Understanding Sexuality

Understanding Addiction

Understanding Creativity

I acknowledge the Yuggera and Ugarapul peoples as the Traditional Owners of the lands and waterways where this book was written. I honour the wisdom that lives within the cultures of our First Nations peoples and celebrate its continuity. I pay my deep respects to Elders past, present and future and send my greatest gratitude for all they do for the life of this land.

Always was, always will be.

Contents

An Important Note

Please do not use this book as a substitute for expert relationship advice. While scientific research will be presented wherever possible, the content is drawn largely from my life experiences and beliefs. I understand that your personal experiences are valuable and unique, and this book is not meant to replace the importance of your own insights in your relationships. Therefore, nothing in this book should be used as professional relationship advice or in place of considered open and compassionate conversations with your loved ones.

If you don't have the skills to have these deep discussions on your own, then please engage the assistance of a qualified therapist or counsellor. These professionals will not only help you work through the questions that arise for you now, but also empower you with vital communication skills that will serve you in good stead in the future. This knowledge will give you the confidence and capability to navigate your relationships more effectively.

Seeking help in your relationships is not a sign of weakness. It is the greatest act of love, care, and respect for yourself and those around you.

Introduction

Like a large segment of the older adult population, I was married for over ten years, but am now divorced. The separation had me reflecting on my original reasons for entering into a marital and monogamous union, but still, after much consideration, my motivations are not entirely clear. When I ask others why they got married, many respond that it was to feel normal or because it was expected of them. I suspect similar pressures influenced my decision. Growing up in a family with strong religious influences, conformity and maintaining social norms were priorities.

Today, however, societal views have evolved significantly. The Church's influence over personal beliefs has diminished, allowing more room to question what is considered 'normal' versus 'natural' for humans. Western societies now support diverse relationship choices, including those of LGBTQ+ individuals. Marriage, or even a traditional relationship, is no longer a prerequisite for having children, thanks to advances in reproductive technology. Moreover, women are increasingly independent, both financially and physically. So, in an era of unprecedented freedom, what role does monogamy play, and why would one choose this form of relationship?

Since becoming single, this question has become more relevant to me. While I enjoy my independence, I still feel societal pressure to return to a traditional, monogamous partnership. There is an underlying expectation that I will seek out someone, 'settle down,' and commit to a conventional couple structure.

This pressure creates an internal conflict: part of me feels drawn to finding another partner, settling down, and embracing the perceived security and stability of monogamy. Media and societal messages often suggest that this is the right path and that diverging from it could lead to ending up a bitter, lonely old cat lady. On the other hand, I am wary of the high divorce rates among those who remarry—65 per cent of second marriages end in divorce, highlighting that many do not learn from their first experience. It raises the question: do we enter new relationships with the same misguided beliefs that led to the breakdown of previous ones?

The saying goes,

> *"The definition of insanity is doing the same thing repeatedly and expecting different results."*

This idea applies to relationships just as much as it does to experiments. Science has a rigorous method of reviewing and reassessing after each experiment. But how often do we, as individuals, take the time to critically evaluate our relationships and the expectations we bring into them? How willing are we to challenge ourselves and adapt during the course of a relationship?

A significant lack of curiosity and reflection about our intimate relationships seems common. Despite the high incidence of family breakdowns, most singles still seek a committed partner and believe in the concept of a soul mate. Statistics show that 89 per cent of singles believe in the possibility of staying married to one person forever, suggesting a strong belief in monogamy as the ideal relationship model. Younger generations often assume they can succeed where their parents failed, believing they have found the secret to lasting monogamy. However, the divorce rates suggest that all of these beliefs are founded on a limited understanding of the inherent challenges of monogamy. As Esther Perel aptly notes,

"We would rather kill a relationship than question its structure."

It appears well past time to question the structure of monogamy. Before choosing to enter a monogamous relationship, it behoves us all to carefully weigh its benefits and drawbacks. As Wayne Dyer reminds us,

"The highest form of ignorance is when you reject something you don't know anything about."

Understanding monogamy fully is essential before deciding to embrace or reject it.

This book aims to explore monogamy in-depth, offering insights that can help us make more informed decisions about its role in our lives and how it aligns with our potential and personal growth. It addresses questions such as:

- What is monogamy?
- Is monogamy natural for humans?
- How did monogamy become the norm?
- What challenges are inherent in monogamy?
- How do love and sex intersect with monogamy?
- What role do childhood influences play in our views on monogamy?
- How do religion and law shape our understanding of relationships?
- Are we truly free to choose monogamy?

A recurring theme in this book is the distinction between what is natural and what is normal. While monogamy may not be natural, it is widely regarded as the standard of morality. Modern media often reinforces this by exposing and shaming infidelity, yet rarely questions why cheating is so prevalent.

When something that is not natural is upheld as normal, conflicts are inevitable—physically, emotionally, psychologically, and spiritually. A deeper understanding of our sexuality and relationship dynamics can reveal why these conflicts occur and why finding a compassionate and practical way through them remains a challenge.

Whether we are genuinely free to choose monogamy is also critical. Simone de Beauvoir suggests that if societal pressures limit our choices, we are not truly free, and feelings of resentment and rebellion are likely. Conversely, suppose we freely choose monogamy but fail to address our concerns or communicate openly. In that case, we may inadvertently mislead our partners, entering a vulnerable arrangement without full transparency.

De Beauvoir further argues that a lifelong commitment can hinder personal growth by limiting our freedom to evolve and seek relationships that better support our development. However, she acknowledges that avoiding commitments altogether has drawbacks, as it can serve as an escape from the challenges of interdependence and vulnerability.

In his book Monogamy, Adam Phillips suggests caution when approaching the topic, implying that those who write about it may be driven by bitterness or fear. While I can confidently say that my reflections on monogamy are not rooted in bitterness, I will attest to feeling a great fear. I am very concerned about repeating past mistakes and perpetuating cycles of hurt. This book is my effort to understand monogamy more fully, not only to avoid future pain but to offer insights that might help others navigate their own paths.

Ultimately, the only way to overcome fear is through understanding. This book explores monogamy and seeks to offer clarity and a foundation for thoughtful decisions about relationships. While there is no one-size-fits-all answer, it encourages readers to consider new models of monogamy that align with human realities and our potential for growth.

By engaging with these ideas, we can hope to transform traditional assumptions and create connections that foster mutual respect, confidence, and personal development.

This book is for anyone questioning the role of monogamy in their life, seeking a deeper understanding of how relationships can support personal fulfilment and the evolution of our society. It is about exploring the intersection of romantic ideals and practical realities and finding ways to align our desires with the truths of our human nature.

As we journey through these pages, may you discover your own expectations and desires around commitment and connection, for it is only through understanding that we can overcome the fears that often overshadow our intimate relationships and find our way to true love.

Chapter 1 – What Is Monogamy?

This chapter aims to bring greater awareness, understanding, and clarity to the words we use to describe our intimate relationships. As you will see, there is no longer a black-and-white world regarding monogamy, but many shades of grey (pardon the pun) comprise this social construct.

As recognised by Gabriel Marcel, some words:

> *"Become charged with passion and so acquire a taboo-value. The thinking which dares to infringe such taboos is considered, if not exactly as sacrilegious, at least as a kind of cheating, or even as something worse."[1]*

Monogamy is one of these taboo words because of its close ties to morality. One only has to look at the synonyms for monogamy to understand its moral weight. Words such as decency, chasteness, devotion, honour, sinlessness, and integrity are all viewed as interchangeable terms for monogamy[2], suggesting that even questioning this concept is considered dirty, evil, and disgraceful.

But how on earth are we to determine whether we want to be "monogamous" if we don't clearly understand what the word implies, and more importantly, whether our personal definition matches that of our partner?

From The Simple...

Many centuries ago, the definition of monogamy was simple and intertwined with marriage. It was true to its Greek origin, where "monos" meant alone and "gamos" meant marriage. Monogamy was then a legally binding marriage to a person of the opposite sex for life[3]. Marriage was deemed a sacred institution, a sacrament, and a contract between the couple and God that could not be broken, even by death.

However, in the mid-1500s, Henry VIII introduced divorce into his new Church of England. Divorce allowed him to keep remarrying until he could get a male heir. The loss of so many people of child-bearing age during centuries of plague also made it a necessity for people to remarry to reproduce and sustain societies. These pressures resulted in a shift in the definition of monogamy from one marriage in a lifetime to one marriage at a time.

The reduced influence of religion has continued over the centuries, and today, less than half of our citizens declare an affiliation with Christianity[4]. This has resulted in significant shifts in the view of marriage and the willingness to enter into it. In 1970, nine per cent of the adult population had never been married, but by 2018, this had jumped to 35 per cent[5]. Over one-third of adults now reject becoming legally bound by marriage. Moreover, where once cohabitation before marriage was seen as "living in sin", now it is commonplace with the vast majority, 88 per cent of couples, live together before marriage[6].

To The Sexual...

The shift in the nature of our intimate relationships away from marriage has also required a broader definition of monogamy. Now, instead of concentrating on the concept of marriage, the definition of monogamy is centred around sex:

"The practice or state of having a sexual relationship with only one partner." (Oxford Languages)

With this definition, though, we enter a very slippery slope. What does a "sexual relationship" mean?

Historically, sexual relations have been defined scientifically as penis-in-vagina intercourse. In our modern world, though, sex is increasingly becoming a function of pleasure rather than procreation, and there are no gender limitations. This simple definition of copulation completely ignores the increased individuality of sexual relations and the vastness of forms they can take.

In themselves, sexual relationships are not simple. The following model of sexuality shows the multitude of ways in which a person can share their sexuality with others. We can do this through talk, touch and the most intimate form of touch, sex. In this model, sex is defined as:

"The act of stimulating the sexual organs of another for pleasure and/or procreation."

Figure 1 - The Components of Sexuality

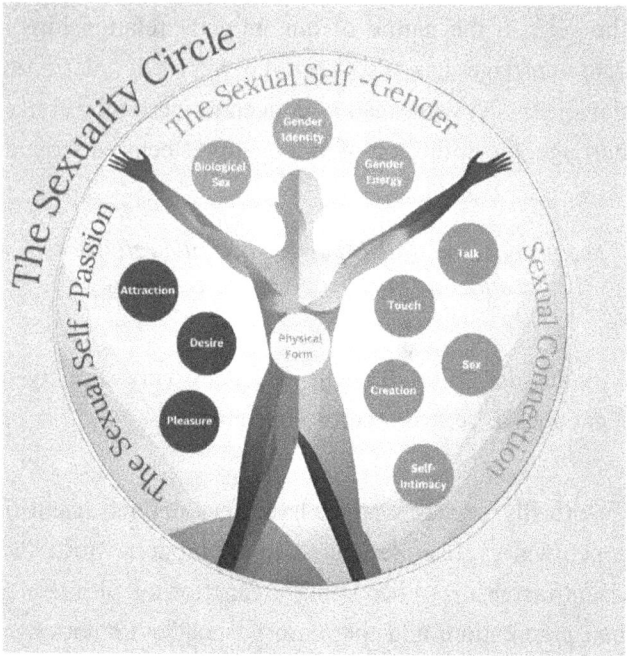

However, as the diagram shows, sex is not the only form of bodily intimacy. There is also a touch of hands, lips, and so many other variations of physical connection that do not involve stimulating the genitalia. And then what about sharing your deepest sexual desires and fears with another? This is also a form of vulnerability and an intermingling of desire and pleasure. One could also argue that the act of creating something with someone is also a form of sexual connection, replicating the joining required for reproduction.

Being close to another person physically usually results from of a plethora of preliminary feelings and choices (either conscious or subconscious). There is generally a sense of attraction to the other's physical and personality characteristics. Normally, there is a desire to touch and be touched by the other person. And there is a sense of pleasure derived from being with the other person.

So, given the layers of sexual connection possible, when does monogamy begin and end? Is monogamy determined by a person's deeds or by their desires? Is it maintained by resisting touch or by resisting thought?

In this way, the concept of monogamy is incredibly complex. While there can be explicit vows that each person will not touch the reproductive organs of another, can the same restrictions be placed on another's words, thoughts, or emotions? How far do the demands of coupledom go into the sexual agency of each person? Where are the boundaries between monogamy and infidelity drawn? What is the perimeter that, once crossed, makes you a cheater?

- Are you a cheater only if you have sex with another person outside the couple?
- What about if you lie naked with them or if you masturbate together?
- Have you been unfaithful if you kiss another person?
- What if you hold their hand?
- How about giving or receiving a massage?
- Are you a cheater if you are attracted to another person?
- Or what if you desperately desire to be close to someone else but don't act on it?

- Are you a cheater if you speak to someone else about your sexual fantasies?

When exactly have you broken the bounds of monogamy?

To The Subjective...

After all of this analysis, we conclude that monogamy, while touted as a set social specification, actually has the potential to be as individual as each of the relationships that bear its name.

As noted by Adam Philips, humans are so desperate for a set of clear and simple rules that:

"We forget how different every couple is."[7]

What is right for one couple may be very different for another. More critically, the beliefs and values of one person in the partnership may be misaligned with the other. They will only know whether they are playing by the same rules if they discuss their explicit expectations.

Suppose you assume that you are both working from the same definition of monogamy. In that case, you may get a nasty surprise and may end up having a conversation that may go something like this:

- "I only kissed her - it's not like I had sex or anything."
- "It was only once – and I have no feelings for him– I promise."

- "Yes, I am incredibly attracted to him – what's wrong with admiring beauty?"
- "Honey I am so sorry, I was drunk, but it was only oral."
- "You are right, I have feelings for him, but I won't ever act on them."

The reality is that while we would love to have clear and simple rules about what monogamy is and what constitutes infidelity, these need to be defined by and for each couple.

There are so many possible and recognised variations of monogamy these days. Reddit chat rooms on relationships are full of people experimenting with different forms and terms for their relationship arrangements. Some options I have encountered include the following:

- Lifetime monogamy – where you only have one sexual partner for life. Traditionalists would argue that this is the only true form of monogamy.
- Serial monogamy – where you only have one sexual partner at a time.
- Social monogamy – where you may have sex with others but maintain a domestic and social arrangement with only one person.
- Reproductive monogamy – where you have sex with others but agree to only breed with one other person.
- Fluid monogamy – where prophylactics protect any sexual activity to prevent sharing bodily fluids.

- Emotional monogamy – where you have sexual relations with others but agree to establish emotional bonds with only one person.

It is interesting that even arrangements that involve sex outside the couple still use the term monogamy to define the relationship. It indicates how deeply monogamy and morality are related in our society and the overwhelming yearning for couples to remain within the moral umbrella of the tribe. It suggests there is so much fear about straying from this gold moral standard that people are weaving words and concepts together to ensure they can still view their relationships as honourable and "normal".

The latter option, emotional monogamy, is the one that, while sounding most innocent, is potentially the most insidious. It seeks to impose constraints on what another person can feel, which is at its best ludicrous and, at its worst, could be described as oppression. Additionally, it can be asserted that the most satisfying of sex is drenched in emotion, and so 'allowing' your loved one to partake in sex outside of the couple but denying them the full experience of it seems like a concession based on control rather than genuine compassion and care for their vitality.

The reality of our world today is that religious and legal authorities have very little influence on how we construct our personal relationships. Each person and couple are free to determine what monogamy means for them.

Therefore, partners must have a shared understanding of what the container of coupledom comprises and how concrete the boundaries may be.

Monogamy is much more complex and individual than any simple definition suggests. So, I will leave you now to consider:

What is your definition of monogamy?

Core Concepts

Monogamy is complex. It is not just one idea; it has many meanings that vary across different relationships.

Monogamy is tied to moral values, making it a sensitive and sometimes taboo topic.

Monogamy carries societal expectations and moral judgments that are hard to escape.

Originally about lifelong marriage, monogamy now often means being sexually exclusive, though what counts as "sexual" can differ greatly.

There are various forms, like lifetime, serial, social, reproductive, fluid, and emotional monogamy, each with its own rules.

Monogamy is a personal construct and can be defined by each couple according to their needs and boundaries.

Couples need to talk openly to ensure they have the same understanding of what monogamy means to them.

It's important for individuals to think about what monogamy means to them and also understand their partner's assumptions and expectations.

Chapter 2 – Is Monogamy Natural?

At its most basic, monogamy is having an exclusive sexual relationship (however you may define it) with one other person. It is certainly the predominant form of relationship structure in society, but is it consistent with human biology? Is monogamy an innate condition for humans or a constructed social convention?

We Are Designed To Reproduce

Despite our intellectual and technological advancements, we must remember that humans are still animals. As much as we like to think we are a superior, enlightened species, our thoughts and actions are still driven by the basic instincts of reproduction[8]. While today, sex may be chosen as a means of pleasure rather than procreation, it does not take away from the millennia of evolution that have shaped us with one purpose in mind—to reproduce.

"In the human species, it (the reproductive instinct) is one of the strongest of the instincts; so strong is it that the control and regulation of its impulse is one of the most difficult problems for the individual and for society."[9]

Monogamy then appears to be somewhat counter to the human instinct for reproduction, limiting the human potential for procreation by:

- Confining men to the reproductive cycle of only one female.
- Preventing men from breeding with other females during a partner's pregnancy.
- Restricting women from maximising their fertile times by accessing sperm from multiple partners and engaging in sperm competition.

Understandably, monogamy would not be a natural choice for animals whose prime priority is to reproduce. Science supports this, with research showing almost all mammals are not monogamous. One study has found that only three per cent of our mammal cousins form pair bonds to rear their young. However, most of these couples also have sex with others outside these pair bonds and so are not a sexually exclusive coupling. The proportion of mammals that maintain sexual exclusivity is much closer to 0.6 per cent[10].

Within our species, only around 21 per cent of global cultures are exclusively monogamous and explicitly outlaw polygamy (where there are multiple spouses for either sex)[11]. Well over three-quarters of the world's cultures, both historically and currently, practice some form of polygyny (the practice of having multiple wives).

Among those communities where monogamy is the sanctioned relationship state, it is reported that at least 40 per cent of men have had an affair during their relationship. This figure is lower for women, with 25 per cent reporting having sex outside their committed relationship[12]. However, this rate is expected to be much higher, with underreporting likely due to the heavier social stigma for women who cheat. Nevertheless, these figures show that monogamy may be the theory behind relationships, but in practice there is a behaviour that appears more polygamous.

In addition, across 160 different societies, it was found that infidelity was by far the most common rationale for ending a marriage[13], with extramarital affairs being the prevalent reason for around 40 per cent of American divorces[14]. Even more interesting, though, is the finding that the vast majority of men (74 per cent) and women (68 per cent) would have an affair if they knew they would never get caught[15]. It appears that without the fear of retribution, most people would quite happily not be monogamous.

As succinctly put by Adam Phillips:

"Not everyone believes in monogamy, but everyone lives as though they do."

Monogamy Is Not In Our Biology

The sperm that men supply during sex is relatively easy to produce and, therefore, a cheap input into the fertilisation process. Because it is plentiful, men can spread it around many women and, as a result there becomes an inherent imperative for men to establish the dominant gene pool. Reproductive success for men, then, is about dominating the gene pool and passing on their DNA to as many offspring as possible. With this goal in mind, there is no advantage to maintaining monogamy, in fact, the opposite, they are driven to copulate with many females and leave a larger genetic legacy[16]. In this way, the males' path to reproductive success is through the quantity of copulation. This desire for genetic dominance is hardwired. However, these days, where men could be required to provide child support for proven offspring, the attractiveness of this approach is significantly lessened.

Women have a much larger investment than men's relatively fleeting contribution to reproduction. They will bear the physical burden of pregnancy for around nine months and the mortal risks of childbirth. If the child is breastfed, the woman will also be responsible for the infant's nourishment for potentially the first few years of its life, tying her to the child. Motherhood is an immense physical and psychological venture. Therefore, each woman needs to ensure they get a good return for their huge investment of time and energy. They want the best offspring possible, which means getting the best sperm. How is this done? Through sperm competition.

You see, women have one adaptation that allows them to game the reproductive system: hidden ovulation. Unlike other animals where the female is obviously in oestrous (on heat), human females have no visible sign. Only the woman, if she observes her mucous throughout the month, can determine when she is most fertile. This clandestine reproductive function gives women immense power to time copulation with several men. It creates a competitive environment where she can ensure the strongest sperm will survive.

In contrast to men, women's strategy for reproductive success is quality – creating the circumstances to get the best possible sperm and, thus, the best possible offspring. The woman's body, too, is well suited to non-monogamy. But women would never be so downright deceitful these days to engage in sperm competition, would they?

The differences in biological imperatives for males and females are outlined in the following table[17].

Figure 2 - Reproduction imperatives of males and females

	Males	**Females**
Inputs	Sperm is plentiful	Eggs are relatively rare
Investment	Low effort and risk in reproduction	High effort and risk in reproduction
Interest	Concerned with creating the dominant gene pool	Concerned with getting strong offspring
Aim	Quantity of copulation to maximise chances of reproductive success	Quality of sperm to ensure the healthiest children

It is in the best interests of both men and women to have sex with multiple partners. Having several sex partners allows the man to work towards establishing the dominant gene pool. It also gives the woman access to the highest quality sperm and, thus, the strongest offspring.

Where the interests between males and females converge is the child's survival. This shared goal makes the creation of pair bonds a logical arrangement. For women, the most obvious bond to be formed is with the child's father, given that his vested interest is more likely to secure the safety and wellbeing of her offspring. And for the father, it is understandable that he will want to provide for the mother and child to ensure they survive to pass on his genes to the next generation. There is certainly a mutuality in maintaining a relationship between the couple.

However, while forming this pair is practical, especially in the children's early years, this does not mean there needs to be sexual exclusivity during this time. It can be argued that parental responsibilities can still be fulfilled without relationship restrictions. Once the offspring are independent and childbearing activities have ceased, there are also no parental responsibilities that would demand the continuation of monogamy in the pair.

Instead, the behavioural ecologist Geoffrey Parker and evolutionary theoretician Robert Trivers have concluded that the best reproductive strategy for humans is a mixed one[18]. They suggest that males and females should create a pair bond for the rearing of offspring but be available for additional copulation if the opportunity arises. This strategy will benefit humanity by ensuring the transmission of the strongest genes and, therefore, creating the healthiest communities.

Our Brains Are Not Wired For Monogamy

One may think that the advanced logical functions of the human brain provide a higher level of morality than those of other animals. Surely, our greater intellect allows us to comprehend the moral failing of infidelity and curb any animalistic urges as they arise. You may be surprised then to learn that the way in which our brains are wired actively supports non-monogamy.

Our brains are programmed to view everything through the lenses of:

- Pleasure. We are compelled to move towards those things that feel good.
- Pain. We will seek to move away from sources of threat or discomfort.

These two basic drivers, pleasure and pain, dictate most, if not all, of our actions.

"Nature has placed humankind under the governance of two sovereign masters, pain and pleasure. It is for them alone to point out what we ought to do, as well as to determine what we shall do." ~ Jeremy Bentham

Our neurology explains why, even though we may be in a loving, committed relationship, we turn our heads to follow someone we find attractive. The pleasure centres are activated well before we have time to think and decide to look away lest we spur the partner's jealousy and wrath. It is these ingrained animal instincts that lead the vast majority of people to admit they would undertake affairs if they did not have to deal with the pain of getting caught. Avoiding pain keeps people faithful, not a biological imperative or innate need to be monogamous.

It is natural for people to move towards those things that bring them pleasure. Sex feels good and, as a bonus, contributes to our genes' survival through reproduction. As stated by Brunning:

"Human behaviour is informed by evolutionary biology and is understood in terms of what best serves the interests of our genes."[19]

In addition to our primal pleasure and pain responses, it has been proven that three separate systems in our brains guide our mating behaviours and intimate relationships[20]. These are the systems of:

1. Sex drive. Creates the impetus to search for a sexual partner.
2. Romantic love. Draws a person in to focus on a potential sexual partner and creates the emotional conditions conducive to sex.
3. Deep attachment. Keeps people together long enough to raise a child.

These systems are not wired together, meaning they can act independently and interact in various combinations. One system does not depend on another.

Figure 3 - The three relational brain systems

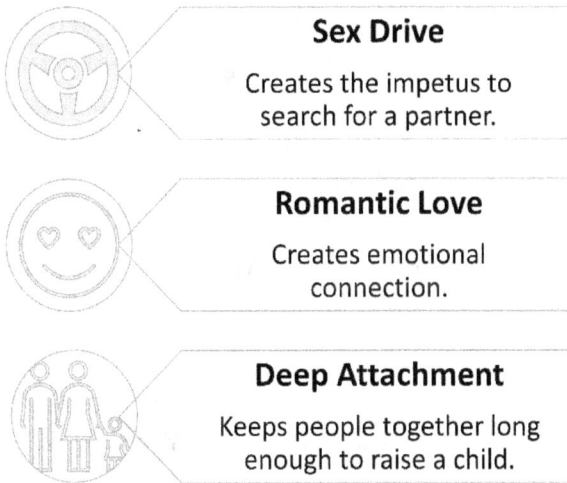

Sex Drive

Creates the impetus to search for a partner.

Romantic Love

Creates emotional connection.

Deep Attachment

Keeps people together long enough to raise a child.

For example, a deep attachment can exist for one person. At the same time, feelings of lust or romance can be felt for another. The sex drive system can also operate in combination with or independently from feelings of romantic love or deep attachment, creating the desire for additional sexual partners beyond these emotional connections. It is, therefore, possible to love your life partner, while still having an impulsive fling with the stranger smiling at you from the other side of the bar. As stated by Helen Fisher:

"Our brain architecture easily accommodates infidelity."

I would go further to say that our brains don't only accommodate infidelity, but are structured in a way that removes the conflict associated with having sexual liaisons outside of the couple. Our brains actually provide a foundation for a mature approach to relationships, recognising our ability to hold love in different ways for different people. However, we have sought to curb this intelligence with rules and strictures around what relationships should look like, and expectations about how a couple should feel towards each other and those around them.

Monogamy As An Evolutionary Tension

Humans have internal and external conditions that we have genetically adapted to over millennia, which have ensured our ability to survive and thrive. These are called Environments of Evolutionary Adaptation (EEA). Mismatches between a person's current setting and an EEA can either have no effect, have a beneficial effect or contribute to mental or physical morbidity. Discrepancies between the optimal and actual conditions that cause negative impacts on physical or mental wellbeing are referred to as discords[21]. Examples of discords already proven include:

- Living in environments devoid of nature. Humans have evolved in close affiliation with nature, with the need to be close to it termed biophilia. Manufactured objects dominate cities and indoor environments, and the absence of natural elements has been found to harm the human mind[22].

- Being raised in core-only families. Growing up in families with only parents and few siblings is correlated with increased mental health issues. Those children who grow up in extended family environments that are more akin to our tribal traditions experience higher levels of mental health.
- The availability of fatty and sugary foods. Genetically, we are wired to prefer high-energy foods such as fats and sugars. These were essential for survival in periods when food was scarce or unpredictable. However, these foods were generally hard to come by in the past, which ensured they were not overconsumed. With fast food's prevalence, these high-energy foods are prolific. Our taste buds, however, have not changed, and we are still naturally drawn to them. It is not surprising then that obesity is a well-recognised disease of modernity.

There is no doubt that monogamous relationships can bring much comfort, companionship, and certainty to life. They can enrich the lives of the couple and all those around them. However, these relationship benefits are not exclusive to monogamy; the same support, confidence, and camaraderie are available through any relationship. And while the benefits of monogamy for social stability and individual integrity are lauded, the dilemmas that arise from its discord with our evolutionary adaptations are not commonly conceded.

Monogamy Is A Social Ideal

Our physical makeup and neural networks are not built to support monogamy. In fact, our bodies and brains largely encourage and support sex outside of a pair bond. So, if monogamy is not ingrained in human biology, it must be purely a social construct. Thus, monogamy is a cultural creation and predominantly a social ideal and is not a natural relationship arrangement for humans.

That monogamy is not natural for humans was recognised way back in the 1930s, when Robert Briffault, in his book Sin and Sex[23], stated that:

"For a male and female to live continuously together is biologically speaking, an extremely unnatural condition."

The less natural our behaviours are, the more difficult they will be to maintain. The further we move away from a natural state, the more tension will arise, and the more fuel is created for conflict. Monogamy then begins to feel less like the happy-ever-after scenarios from the Disney Princess movies we watched as a child and much more like the Shawshank Redemption.

"The further the gap between what is natural and what is normal, the more torment and tension there will be." ~
Belinda Tobin

However, just because monogamy may not be natural, nor in line with human biological imperatives, it is a relationship structure that many people hold dear and have inscribed into their core value system. This chapter has not sought to contest this but simply allow people to understand and prepare for the challenges that may arise with this choice. Knowing that monogamy is unnatural will allow us greater insight into difficulties in an exclusive partnership arrangement and provide the potential for caring responses.

Core Concepts

Monogamy is not consistent with human biology, which is driven by the goal of maximising reproduction and sustaining the species.

Most animals, including mammals, are not monogamous, and only a tiny fraction practice sexual exclusivity.

Men are biologically inclined to spread their genes widely, while women seek the best genetic material through hidden ovulation and sperm competition.

Both sexes benefit from multiple partners: men for quantity, women for quality.

In human societies, monogamy is not universal, with many cultures allowing polygamy. Even in monogamous societies, infidelity is common.

Pair bonds between parents help with child-rearing, but they don't necessarily require sexual exclusivity. Researchers suggest the most successful strategy is a mixed one; forming pair bonds for child-rearing but allowing additional sexual partners to maximise reproductive quantity and quality.

The brain systems for sex drive, romantic love, and deep attachment are separate, allowing for these things to occur simultaneously.

Monogamy is largely a social ideal, not a natural state for humans. It is expected then that monogamy will come with torment and tension.

Chapter 3 – Monogamy Through The Lens Of The Natural Laws

The previous chapter presented science showing monogamy as an unnatural mating arrangement for humans, as it inhibits our reproductive potential. Choosing monogamy means understanding our minds and bodies may work against it, with natural conflicts arising. Beyond biology, however, monogamy can be examined against the pervasive rhythms of natural laws—the principles governing every aspect of life. These are known as the Universal, Natural or Hermetic Laws.

The Universal Laws

The Seven Hermetic Laws were named after their creator Hermes Trismegistus, who was revered as a god of wisdom in the first century AD. They are said to govern the operation of every living being, our planet, and the universe. While they were considered both blasphemous and heretical at the time, centuries later they became vital inputs to the transformational philosophies of the Renaissance. Nowadays, these laws are entrenched in the plethora of self-development teachings covering attraction, manifestation, and self-mastery. If you were to look closely at the celebrated teachings of Tony Robinson, Zig Ziglar, Eckhardt Tolle, Deepak Chopra and even the Dalai Lama you will see how they are built upon these universal laws. Even our modern-day psychological systems draw from aspects of these inescapable truths.

The original seven laws are:
1. Mentalism – The All is mind; The universe is mental.
2. Correspondence - As above, so below; As below, so above. As within, so without; As without, so within.
3. Vibration - Nothing rests; Everything moves; Everything vibrates.
4. Polarity - Everything has poles; Everything has its pair of opposites; Opposites are identical in nature but different in degree.
5. Rhythm - The pendulum swing manifests in everything; The measure of the swing to the right is the measure of the swing to the left.
6. Cause and effect - Every cause has its effect; Every effect has its cause.
7. Gender - Gender is in everything; Everything has its masculine and feminine principles; Gender manifests on all planes.

The theory is that to function in alliance with these laws brings peace, wisdom and prosperity. Operating in ignorance and opposition to these principles brings tension and turmoil. So how well does our modern view of monogamy foster the former and prevent the latter?

Monogamy is mental – The universe is mental

"There is nothing either good or bad but thinking makes it so."~ William Shakespeare

The principle of mentalism suggests that our experiences are shaped by our thoughts—mental constructs that influence our reality. Because our minds create our circumstances, we have the power to change them by adjusting our perceptions.

Monogamy, likewise, is not a biological necessity but a social construct. The belief that monogamy is ideal, or that it inherently reflects morality, is only a thought shared by some cultures, not a universal truth. Other communities hold different beliefs, creating alternative relationship norms.

It is also merely a thought that infidelity equates to a lack of love, despite evidence showing that love and sexual desire can operate independently. Mentalism implies that we cannot fully understand our or another's mind; most of our thoughts occur subconsciously, meaning that even in close relationships, full understanding is elusive.

This principle challenges monogamy by showing that we can never entirely know our partner's inner world. This reality can lead either to suspicion or to empathy and resilience. We choose whether to treat relationships as risk management or as a respectful acknowledgment of each other's complex minds.

Mentalism also offers opportunities for monogamous relationships. By examining our beliefs about monogamy, we can reshape them to foster healthier, more compassionate connections. Since monogamy is a mental construct, we can tailor it to reflect our personal values and the natural laws, allowing monogamy to be whatever we choose it to be.

Coupledom and Correspondence- As above, so below

"The outer conditions of a person's life will always be found to reflect their inner beliefs." ~ James Allen

The principle of correspondence describes how the quality of our lives depends on the quality of our thoughts and that changing our life trajectory also requires a change in our beliefs.

Figure 4 - The Cognitive Behavioural Therapy Model

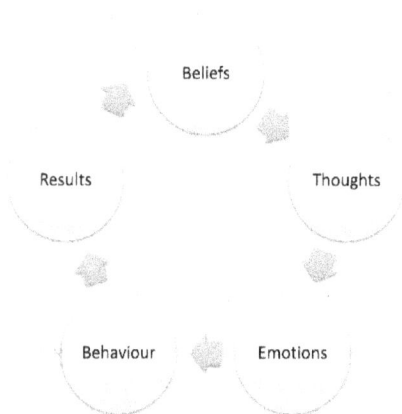

Beliefs

Results

Thoughts

Behaviour

Emotions

The CBT model shows the process by which our beliefs become self-fulfilling prophecies. Our beliefs begin a whole chain of thoughts, feelings, and actions, the outcome of which is then used to confirm or contest the beliefs that beget them. Sometimes it is easier to see how this all works through an example. So here is one I prepared earlier!

For instance, if you believe true love means never desiring anyone else, then feeling attracted to another person may trigger guilt, anxiety, and even behavioural changes. You may be afraid that you have fallen out of love with your partner and are bad for even thinking about infidelity. You might overcompensate in your relationship or withdraw socially, which can lead to suspicion and isolation. Hiding away will not necessarily reduce the desires but will create boredom and loneliness, which may work to fuel other fires. Either way, the belief that having desires for someone other than your partner is bad has led to other destructive outcomes, being the birth of suspicion or the association of monogamy with isolation and insipidness.

There is an alternative cycle, though, that goes like this. In contrast to the previous belief, say this time you believe it is natural to be sexually attracted to people other than your partner. When the thought arises that you would love to have sex with that other person, there is no surprise. Instead of the shame that arose previously, you can celebrate the fact that you still feel the vitality of desire and that you can appreciate beauty. The result of this situation is that monogamy has no effect on your social life and is not a source of tension between the couple. In this circumstance, the belief has created space for the sexual desire of others within the pair. This experience then confirms the belief that it is possible to be sexually attracted to other people and still love your partner.

As these simple and somewhat idealistic examples illustrate, the beliefs we hold around exclusive sexual relationships ignite a string of explosive expectations about our own and our partner's behaviour. Put simply, your beliefs about monogamy will create your experience of it.

The Vibrating Twosome- Nothing rests

"Change is inevitable. Growth is optional." ~ John C. Maxwell

The law of vibration, echoing the Buddhist law of impermanence, emphasizes that change is inevitable and stability is illusory. Physically, we change daily, with billions of cells replaced, and this state of flux applies equally to our mental and emotional worlds, including relationships.

James Hillman suggests that constancy in commitment is unrealistic:

"Such an arrangement can't hold because life wants to break in on that deathly demand for absolute stability."

Our biology also drives relationship changes; as Helen Fisher notes, hormones fuelling romance only last a few years. George Bernard Shaw recognized this natural decline in passion, observing that romantic intensity is inherently short-lived.

Feelings toward an intimate partner are bound to shift, as are relationship needs. Some may cling to novelty, while others seek stability. The introduction of no-fault divorce reflects society's acknowledgment that relationships often evolve in ways that lead to "irreconcilable differences."

The real question isn't whether relationships will change but whether monogamy can allow each partner the freedom to grow. Relationships that are too rigid eventually stagnate. Embracing vibration within monogamy offers couples the chance to develop individually and create a flexible arrangement that enables both partners to flourish.

Polarity and the Pair- Everything has its pair of opposites

Everything has an opposite; nothing exists without its antithesis. Joy is understood through sadness, warmth through coldness, and peace through war. Adam Phillips highlights this duality in monogamy:

"Monogamy comes with infidelity built in, if only as a possibility."

Where monogamy exists, the potential for infidelity also exists, making fidelity a continual choice and commitment.

Modern relationships often view success as merging completely with a partner—sharing activities, preferences, and social circles. Divergence can be seen as division, leading partners to lose individuality in pursuit of unity. What is not often considered in the pursuit of unification is the energy created by the attraction of opposites. Instead of a dance of individual energies and the excitement of the unknown, the monogamous couple often drifts towards the centre, where there is no movement – only stagnation.

This situation is highlighted by Simone de Beauvoir, who argues that attraction comes from there being a separate, distinct and different "other". She suggests that in the pursuit of monogamy, the couple becomes the same; thus, curiosity and desire are lost. Monogamy then seems to want to ignore the dynamic principle of polarity in favour of solidity and settling.

There is another element of this principle that is also important for monogamous relationships, and that is how we may seek to have our opposing needs satisfied by one chosen partner. Humans are complex creatures, and while we may crave spontaneous stimulation and sensual surprise, we also have an innate need for safety and security and to feel comfortable and confident in the arms of our companions. We expect the other to be our partner in dirty domestic chores as well as the satisfier of our sexual desires. One could also assert that it is completely selfish and downright disrespectful to expect one person to satisfy the entire scope of our divergent needs. It places enormous pressure on someone else to be your "everything". While we tend to expect that our partner will meet all these opposing expectations, we are quick to exclaim that they are unrealistic if they propose we should do the same for them. Such is the "hypocrisy of the conjugal life."

The Rhythmic Duo- The pendulum swing manifests in everything

The principle of polarity shows us that opposites exist in everything, while the principle of rhythm indicates continual movement between these contrasts. The pendulum illustrates this movement, where swinging to one extreme inevitably leads to an opposite swing.

In monogamy, rhythm's effect depends on how tightly exclusivity is defined. If monogamy is enforced in extreme terms—expecting a partner not even to feel attraction for others—the principle of rhythm suggests this rigidity can lead to a counter-swing toward liberation or secretive behaviours. Esther Perel highlights how this movement may manifest:

"Affairs, online encounters, strip clubs, and sex on business trips are common transgressions that establish psychological distance from an overbearing relationship."

The principle of rhythm also tells us that our needs swing between the poles over time. We can move radically and rapidly from feelings of great selflessness to a drive for selfishness and self-satisfaction. Sometimes we can shift in seconds from the intense pull towards security and stability to a burning desire to run wild and free and seek all of life's adventures. These internal fluctuations can cause us to feel conflicted, even questioning our ability to find satisfaction in monogamy. Sometimes these shifts are rapid, but often they take years, leading to introspection and self-criticism.

In essence, rhythm reveals that alternating emotions and desires are natural. Just as waves rise and fall, feelings of love and attraction ebb and flow, making it unsurprising if we experience moments of conflict in monogamy. Assuming relationships are unchanging sources of stability is unrealistic. In sum, "we are all naturally swingers!"

The Cause and Effect of Connection- Every cause has its effect

"Garbage in, garbage out."

The law of cause and effect tells us that every situation we encounter has a source, and every action we take has a consequence. This may seem like a simplistic proposition, but its implications are immense. For example, your decision to enter into a monogamous relationship is not just a random occurrence but a result of many internal and external contributors. You may like to think of it as an independent and considered decision, whereas it is more likely to be based on a complex set of preceding conditions.

Within the relationship itself, the quality of inputs each individual brings determines the quality of the connection. As you will see later in the book, there is one key input into relationships that has a significant consequence. It is whether the relationship is entered into from a place of love, or fear. Are you entering an exclusive relationship because you believe it is true to your nature and best for the wellbeing of yourself and your partner? Or is the decision driven by concern about losing the person if you don't commit, or how the many couples in your social sphere may view you?

The drivers of your decision are essential considerations because the inputs' quality determines the effect's quality, or as the techies say, garbage in, garbage out. If it is love that you bring into the choice of monogamy, then it is love that you will receive. If it is fear that is your prime motivation, then it is fear that will haunt your relationship.

Gender Balance - Everything has it's masculine and feminine

The principle of gender builds on polarity, emphasizing that masculine and feminine energies exist in all things and work together to create vitality. This doesn't mean males have only masculine energy and females only feminine; rather, this law states that everyone and everything embodies both energies, which ideally work in harmony. The ultimate aim is to have both energies working together to ignite life.

Masculine energy is assertive, logical, and goal-oriented, driving progress and solutions. Feminine energy, by contrast, nurtures, values relationships, and flows fluidly rather than focusing on outcomes. When balanced, these energies create life-affirming vitality. However, an imbalance can lead to challenges: too much masculine energy makes life feel like constant work, while excess feminine energy can lead to a lack of structure and focus.

There is no doubt our modern lives are masculine-heavy. Our days are filled with making plans, following rules and solving problems. We are driven by science and logic, with little room for spirituality and intuition. We are so busy operating in the world of work that there is very little time for nurturing and investments in our relationships. The reality is that we end up with both partners operating from the masculine energy. It is no wonder, then, that our relationships end up feeling draining and devoid of purpose.

What does this mean for monogamy? It means that for monogamy to work in our materialistic culture, the couple needs to resist the masculine rule of their relationship by being:

- Cognisant that both energies are required.
- Vulnerable and safe enough to express each energy.

It takes considerable insight and courage to negotiate roles for each partner around the masculine and feminine energies, yet this is required if the couple wants to keep the relationship alive.

The Profound Potential of the Principles

This analysis shows that there is nothing in the natural laws that would preclude monogamy from flourishing. What it does illustrate though are the conditions necessary for a sexually exclusive arrangement to thrive. For a monogamous relationship to minimise tension and conflict within and among each participant, it will need to:

- Have alignment between the beliefs upon which the monogamous union is based and the natural human state.
- Embed compassion for the complex, subconscious and changeable nature of each person's needs.
- Encourage development of each individual to ensure the continual improvement of relationship inputs.
- Create space for flux, independence and separateness.
- Celebrate and foster the flow of both masculine and feminine energies.

Many of these preconditions are counter to the traditional view of monogamy, which is based on flawed notions of fidelity, is positioned as a sanctum of stability, and is lauded as an act of completion for two imperfect individuals. While our biology may make monogamy incredibly challenging, it appears a great deal difficulty also arises from the beliefs we bring into it and the choices we make for how it is constructed.

Core Concepts

Monogamy can be examined through the universal principles, known as the Hermetic or Natural Laws.

Mentalism: Monogamy is a mental construct.

Correspondence: Our beliefs about monogamy will shape our experiences of it.

Vibration: Change is inevitable and so monogamy must allow for personal growth and adaptation.

Polarity: Opposites coexist. Balancing intimacy and autonomy sustain attraction.

Rhythm: Needs fluctuate. Monogamy must be flexible to respect these rhythms.

Cause and Effect: The motivation for entering a monogamous union shapes its quality.

Gender Balance: Harmonizing masculine and feminine energies within the relationship enhances vitality and connection.

Aligning monogamous relationships with natural laws allows for flexibility, mutual growth, and a sustainable partnership.

Chapter 4 – How Did Monogamy Become Normal?

We have seen that monogamy is not ingrained in human physiology or neurology. Yet, in Western cultures, there is a monomania around monogamy. This one relationship idea has been determined as more valuable than any other. Monogamy has been crowned as the moral superior of relationship models. However, if you dig into history, it is clear that the presumption of sexual exclusivity within a couple is a relatively modern arrangement.

The Ancient and Middle Ages

In ancient civilisations, the marital home was expected to portray the height of purity and civility. Sex among the married couple was geared towards reproduction, with lust, love or passion believed to pollute the wholesomeness of the union. Yet it was understood that sexual passion was a natural state that, if suppressed, would create dangerous instability in society. So, while procreation was expected only within the marriage, extra-marital sexual exploits for men were expected, accepted and even supported by the state. This division between the purity of the pair and the passion endorsed outside the marriage is represented by the views of the philosopher Seneca:

"Nothing is more impure than to love one's wife as if she were a mistress."[24]

Men in Ancient Greece and Rome were provided with several ways to alleviate their desire for sexual variety, including with slaves, Hetairas and concubines. The open availability of sexual and sensual supplements to their wives meant that the males in these cultures were very "comfortably polygamous"[25]. It also meant that the stock of potential wives was kept pure.

With the prominence of Christianity, the seventh commandment– though shall not commit adultery – became the ruling order. And so, while prostitution was accepted as a necessary evil, married men were technically not allowed to use their services. However, how strongly this commandment was enforced varied depending on the level of wealth involved. The pope crowned Charlemagne the Holy Roman Emperor in 800 even though he was well-known for demonstrating little "Christian piety in his sexual or marital behaviour"[26]. In the twelfth and thirteenth centuries, adultery was openly advocated as the "highest form of love in the aristocracy." If you were wealthy and were not having affairs, then there was just not enough love in your life. How incredibly opposite this view is to our modern insular view of devotion!

In the Middle Ages, similar to the situation in ancient cultures, sex with a spouse was a function of procreation, and passion was to be found in the arms of other lovers. It was unusual for men to have sexual encounters with their wives after the childrearing was complete. Clergy were also embroiled in corruption of the Christian commandments, with many being married and having mistresses. For example, Pope Alexander VI, who ruled the Catholic Church in the late 1400s, had several mistresses during his reign. However, historical records show that he confessed on his deathbed and was surely forgiven for his sins!

The hypocrisy of those in religious power was a motivating force behind the Reformation and the establishment of Protestantism. The other was Henry VIII's shifting sentiments towards his wives and Anne Boleyn's insistence that she would not have sex with him until they were married. In this case, an entire religion was created to support new rules around intimate unions that benefited the King.

While non-monogamy was normal, it is fair to say that it was the right of the rich. Concubines, mistresses and masters were a status symbol that indicated wealth, not only in monetary form but also in the availability of leisure time. Keeping courtesans could be expensive. There were gifts to give and attention required to retain their favour. It is hard to imagine the peasants working at the piggeries having the resources to invest in infidelity. Aristocracy also had another important resource: its relationship with the Church. Their financial support of the Church ensured God's representatives granted them favours and forgiveness.

And, of course, it can be asserted that non-monogamy was also normal for men but rare for women. While there are records describing powerful women taking lovers, their pivotal role in providing heirs meant they were more likely to be controlled and chained up with chastity belts[27] rather than allowed courtesans. Most famously, Guinevere paid the ultimate price for her pursuit of love outside her marriage to Arthur, and Anne Boleyn was beheaded based on accusations of adultery.

Right up until the late 1700s, love was seen to be such a fickle emotion that to marry under the influence of it was viewed as stupid and was grounds for banishment and withdrawal of inheritance[28]. Marriage was not used as a public display of devotion but was predominantly a tool for economic advancement. For the upper class, marriage served a political and social function, forming alliances and combining assets to grow the influence and wealth of both parties. Reproduction ensured the continued reign of their dynasty and the opportunity to make further advantageous allegiances through their children.

For the poorer classes, marriage was more of a mechanism for survival. Men and women needed the support of each other to till fields and run the trade and artisan businesses that provided their income. Procreation was essential to provide business labour and assist the ageing couple. In this way, regardless of stature, marriage was a function of logic and pragmatism, not of love and passion. These latter pleasures were to be found outside of marriage or not had at all.

The Shift Towards Monogamy

So, what changed? When did society begin to focus on the sexual exclusivity of the (married) couple? When did monogamy become the gold standard of morality?

To go through all the events in this evolution would easily fill several books and distract from the intention of this chapter. To keep it simple, I will focus on the three key societal changes that have shaped the current expectations of monogamy. These three influences are:

- The joining of love and marriage in the Age of Romanticism (late 18th to the end of the 19th century).
- The rise of Industrialism and the prominence of private property (late 19th century).
- The transition from tribes to an insular family unit (20th century onwards).

Love And Marriage

The Age of Romanticism was focused on appreciating and expressing human emotions. Just as the Age of Enlightenment placed extreme faith in science and logic, the Age of Romanticism pushed the pendulum back towards the importance of our feelings. In this era, we see a marriage's politics and practicalities intertwined with and finally overtaken by the notions of love.

In Pride and Prejudice, published in 1813, one of literature's great heroines, Elizabeth Bennet, declares that:

"I am determined that only the deepest love will induce me into matrimony."

A few centuries before, it was deemed idiotic to marry for love. However, under Romanticism, it was the height of lunacy to consider entering a relationship without it. As a result, love, which was previously pursued outside the marriage, was best found within. Love was not a nice extra to marriage, it became essential.

Passionate sex was previously associated with love (yes, the Sex Trap is centuries old) but was meant to be found outside the constant and calm coupledom. Now, though, this love was to be brought within the marriage, and the expectations around sex came with it. Instead of having different homes for the opposing needs of stability and passion, all desires were now to be met within the family, united under the umbrella of love. This transition is displayed in the diagrams below.

Figure 5 - Monogamy before and after Romanticism

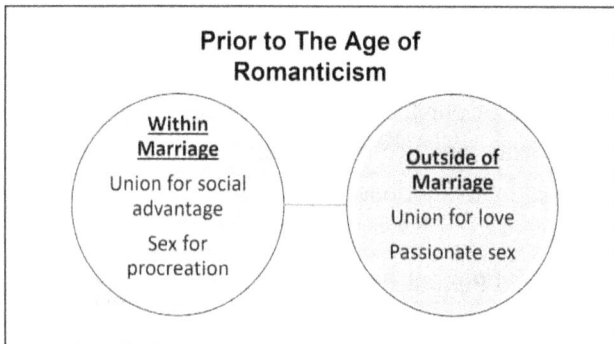

Prior to The Age of Romanticism

Within Marriage
Union for social advantage
Sex for procreation

Outside of Marriage
Union for love
Passionate sex

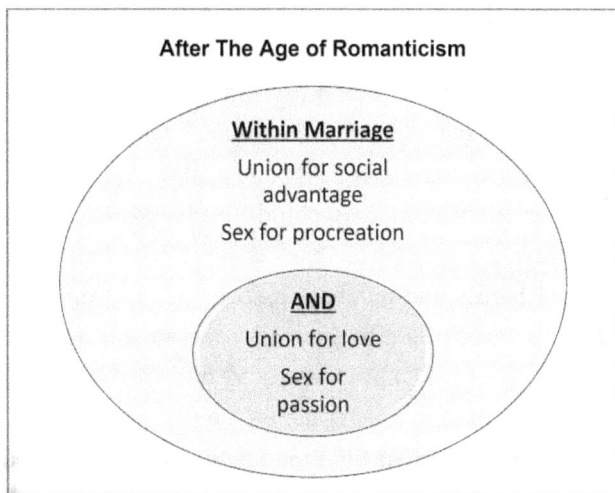

This is where we see the very first use of the word monogamous. While the noun monogamy was in use from the 1600s, the adjective monogamous only appeared in 1770. With the Age of Romanticism, sexual exclusivity began to be used as an attribute by which people described themselves and which could be used to distinguish themselves from others. Now, people could be classified and criticised for this item of identity.

Given love was now essential to coupledom, then fidelity also became non-negotiable. It became unacceptable to stray as adultery became an indicator that you no longer loved your partner. And if love no longer existed there was no reason to stay together. Divorce was very well accepted then (thanks to Henry VIII). Hence, the solution to lost love was to divorce and seek revived passion in a new marriage. Does this sound familiar?

The Rise of Private Property

At the same time that love was at the forefront of relationships, the Industrial Revolution was in full swing, bringing a new wave of equality and egalitarianism to society. With industrialisation, men could find work in factories and gain access to a regular income. This income could finance a wife and family and purchase assets such as property. Now that more men could afford wives, governments had to make sure they could all have access to one. Too many lonely young men with too much time on their hands does not bode well for societal order. So, monogamy was a way to ensure equal access to wives and, by proxy, sexual satisfaction and social stability.

Additionally, with regular incomes, more people could save and purchase property and other physical assets. The more you have, though, the more you have to protect. It had always been imperative to have a clear line of inheritance to property and power. Still, instead of being a concern only for the wealthy, the purity of heirs became a consideration for the middle class. As we have seen, monogamy is a critical mechanism for the maintenance of pure lines of succession and for preventing hard-earned assets from being lost to illegitimate children[29].

In this context, adultery was seen both as a sign of lovelessness and as theft of assets. Both man and wife were responsible for creating heirs that would care for the complete stock of family possessions. When one strayed and created children outside this bond, then claims could be made that splintered their hard-earned wealth and sacrificed it to outsiders, considered akin to destroying the couple's property and stealing from the valid beneficiaries. For these reasons, adultery became a crime in many Western nations and is still punishable in several US states.

The Move To An Insular Family Unit

The combination of The Age of Romanticism and Industrialism created a very peculiar outcome, best shown by Maslow's hierarchy of needs. Industrialism lifted the living standards of many Western nations and provided the means to attain private property. As the need for safety was increasingly satisfied, people were free to seek intimacy and connection. People could focus on finding love, building a family (love and belonging) and raising their reputation as upstanding and credible citizens (Esteem).

Figure 6 - Maslow's Hierarchy of Needs

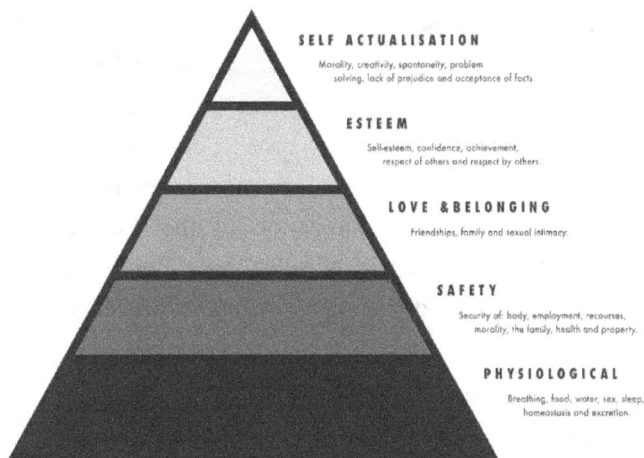

SELF ACTUALISATION
Morality, creativity, spontaneity, problem solving, lack of prejudice and acceptance of facts.

ESTEEM
Self-esteem, confidence, achievement, respect of others and respect by others.

LOVE & BELONGING
Friendships, family and sexual intimacy.

SAFETY
Security of: body, employment, recourses, morality, the family, health and property.

PHYSIOLOGICAL
Breathing, food, water, sex, sleep, homeostasis and excretion.

Esteem is now the key focus for many. As a result, everything that came before self-esteem has been transformed into tools to boost an individual's sense of identity and standing in society. An individual's job, physical possessions and fitness are all used as status symbols to signify success. Similarly, the person's family becomes a possession and a resource that can be used to reinforce individual status. A healthy brood of children becomes a testament to the individual's fertility and virility. And thanks to the link between love and fidelity, a faithful partner indicates the presence of love and, even more importantly, validates the person's worthiness to be loved. With a preoccupation on Esteem, a cheating spouse becomes the ultimate shame, for it suggests that you are in some way deficient.

Through Industrialism and the new religion of materialism, the couple has become an insular unit, bonded to build wealth and support each other's self-esteem. Increasingly, couples are comprised of individuals who have moved away from family units to seek success. So, the support once received from a caring community now needed to be found within their own four walls. A person's inner worth is no longer determined by their role in a broader community. It is pegged to the reciprocal love of their partner. If their relationship falls apart, so does the foundation of their self-esteem and, ultimately, their sense of self-worth. Removing Maslow's brick of Love and Belonging means that Esteem also comes tumbling down.

And this is at the heart of why monogamy has become so serious. We depend on our partners for all our needs - safety, love, belonging and esteem. Thanks to the romantics, we also link fidelity with love and adultery with lack of love. Therefore, if our partners remain faithful, then they love us and then we can assume that we are worth loving, and our self-esteem stays intact. However, suppose our partner cheats on us. In that case, we may assume it is because they don't love us, which also causes us to question whether we are worthy of love at all. And this is why infidelity creates so much hurt and confusion. It is not necessarily about what our partner did, but what their actions potentially say about us.

Materialism and individualism have created insular family units where our 'everything' depends on one person. When all our eggs are in one basket, dropping the basket will create an almighty mess. Fear of this mess is ever-present, and much effort is invested in protecting the basket. In this way, I think it is not love that is the motivation to maintain monogamy, but fear - fear of losing financial support, social status and connections, self-esteem, and self-worth. Monogamy is a way we try to mitigate these risks and, once a tool for protecting assets, is now a means of protecting our self-esteem.

What Is Normal Today?

With regard to intimate relationships, it is normal that:
- People will have been promiscuous (potentially non-monogamous) before pledging sexual exclusivity.
- Each individual in the couple will expect the other to be faithful to them.

- The couple equates the other's ability to remain faithful as an indicator of love.
- While in the relationship, most people will have the desire to cheat.
- Around half of the relationships will dissolve, with separation occurring on average after eight years and divorce after 12 years[30].
- Infidelity will be the likely cause of the relationship breakdown.
- The aggrieved partner will blame the relationship's failure on their partner's inability to uphold the expectation of monogamy rather than question the expectation itself.
- The 'cheater' will feel like a failure due to their inability to quell their natural desires and uphold the gold standard of modern morality.

What is glaringly absent in this picture of normality is the expectation of infidelity. Despite all the statistics showing the prevalence of desired or actual adultery, no one is saying they expect infidelity. They expect monogamy, which has a 50 per cent success rate. And yet they don't also expect infidelity, which is a key cause of the 50 per cent failure rate.

I'm sorry. Is it just me, or does this state of normality sound absurd? The current state of 'normal' monogamy is a fragile façade covering a tumultuous state of tension. Monogamy could be likened to the Titanic – the unsinkable moral standard – one that will never let us down. But the fact is, when we look at the normal state of monogamy today, it is letting us down badly. People are drowning in despair because of broken promises and doubting themselves when they fail to fit the expectation of exclusivity. As Esther Perel states:

> *"Despite the fact that monogamy is a ship sinking faster than anyone can bail it out, we continue to cling to the wreckage with absolute faith in its structural soundness."*[31]

As Michele Scheinkman outlines, people are more tolerant of engaging in the destructive processes of divorce than of having constructive conversations about the reality of our human relationships.

> *"American culture has great tolerance for divorce – where there is total breakdown of the loyalty bond and painful effects for the whole family – but it is a culture with no tolerance for sexual infidelity."*

It appears that what is normal is living in the delusion that monogamy is working for us in its current form.

Core Concepts

Historically, monogamy as sexual exclusivity has not been the norm. Marriages were focused on reproduction, while passion and sex outside marriage were widely accepted, especially for wealthy men who could afford mistresses and concubines.

The idea of monogamy as a moral standard began to take shape during the Age of Romanticism (late 18th to 19th centuries) when love and marriage became linked.

Before this, marriage was more about economic or social alliances than romantic love and it was seen as ludicrous to marry for a feeling as fickle as love.

The Industrial Revolution further shaped monogamy by promoting private property and the need for clear lines of inheritance.

Industrialisation and materialism shifted focus to the nuclear family, moving away from broader community ties. Couples became insular units, relying heavily on each other for emotional and financial support, increasing the pressure to maintain monogamy.

Monogamy has become linked to self-esteem and societal status. As a result, fidelity is equated with personal worth, and infidelity is seen as a personal failure and a sign of little self-worth.

Chapter 5 – The Morality of Monogamy

Morals are a behavioural code of conduct we prescribe for ourselves and use to form relationships with others. While they are predominantly individual decisions, they are shaped by the society in which we live. Our parents are the first teachers of what is right and wrong, and we learn to appreciate the comfort that comes with conformance. As we grow, societal norms also have a strong hold over our behavioural choices, with very few of us courageous enough to risk bearing the title of deviant.

This way, having a social set of behavioural standards across society has many advantages. Morality can create strong communities based on shared values and an agreed set of acceptable behaviours. Moreover, it can contribute to consistency and stability for all its citizens. A great sense of safety and security comes from knowing what to expect from those around you. Boundaries of behaviour are clear, and the community can enforce these effectively through the tools of shame and guilt. If legislated, remedy for breaches is also possible through legal action.

Conforming to mainstream morals also makes each person's life easier. Individuals don't have to do the hard work of self-reflection and creating their own character[32]. They save this trouble by picking one off the shelf that society has already created for them.

However, for all of its benefits, morality also has its shortcomings. While it can create compassionate communities, it can also isolate individuals and divide them through differences.

Severe standards repress the reality and richness of personal complexity and inhibit individuality. The lack of tolerance for diversity can also significantly impede effective decision-making. As acknowledged by Stuart Mills[33], men are imperfect creatures and cannot see all sides of the truth. Rejecting alternative moralities then also limits comprehensive considerations and credible outcomes.

Morality, while having the potential to bring people together under a common set of values, can also create division and disruption. Morals often focus on what a group already has in common, which is a restrictive view based on current circumstances. It is less used to spur conversations about what people would like to have in common, which creates the potential for broader, more inclusive communities. For example, holding onto the moral of monogamy makes polygamists different and thus dangerous. But what if the focus instead was on the mutual desire to create and sustain loving and respectful relationships? A less granular view of morality may allow meeting on common ground and advancing actions that benefit a much wider proportion of the population.

Additionally, the less realistic and more rigid the morals are, the greater the likelihood of a radical recoil. Instincts and desires do not diminish just because we are told that they are not "right". Instead, those things condemned by society may find other, less public channels for expression, or may be held within, toxifying the host and causing more harmful behaviours. Perhaps this is one of the reasons for the popularity of porn. It provides a convenient way to role-play fantasies not possible in a bonded relationship, if only in people's imaginations.

"Morality has hardly made us better people; but it has certainly enriched our vices"[34]

The Moral Dilemmas of Monogamy

The social psychologist Jonathan Haidt has identified six innate moral foundations formed from our evolutionary adaptive challenges. These are shown in the following table.

Figure 7 - The six moral foundations

Moral Foundation	Adaptive Challenge	Characteristic Emotions
Liberty / oppression	Noticing and preventing dominance	Reactance and resentment
Care / harm	Protect and care for children	Compassion
Fairness / cheating	Reap benefits of two-way partnerships	Anger, gratitude, guilt

Moral Foundation	Adaptive Challenge	Characteristic Emotions
Loyalty / betrayal	Form cohesive coalitions	Group pride, rage at traitors
Authority / Subversion	Forge beneficial relationships within hierarchies	Respect, fear
Sanctity / degradation	Avoid contaminants	Disgust

Interestingly, those with liberal political leanings tend to focus on the first three foundations (liberty, care and fairness). In contrast, those with conservative views apply all five to their decision-making. It was also identified that the prime drivers for libertarians are curiosity, experimentation and experience. In comparison, those on the far right are motivated predominantly by fear.

A moral dilemma arises when:

- A person needs to make a decision.
- There are multiple courses of action to choose from.
- No matter what action is taken, some moral foundation will be compromised.

Put simply, a moral dilemma is a situation with no perfect solution. Whatever decision is made will go against one of your values. In this way, there is no logical or rational methodology for resolving this dilemma. Choosing a solution will involve confusion, uncertainty and compromise.

Let's examine the dilemmas that may arise for those entering and working to sustain a monogamous relationship.

The Expectation Of Monogamy

Dilemmas can begin the moment when one or both partners begin to get serious about committing to each other. Suppose monogamy becomes a relationship condition, either determined explicitly, or assumed by one or both parties. In that case, the relationship is based upon the moral foundations of fairness, loyalty to the partnership and respect for the monogamous tradition. However, simultaneously, you will have chosen against the foundations of liberty and potentially care for individual needs. In this way, the initial expectation of monogamy in the couple has already created tension. The couple can celebrate the choice made but forget that one day, the foundation of liberty they forewent may come back to haunt them.

"Unexpressed emotions will never die. They are buried alive and will come forth later in uglier ways." ~ Sigmund Freud

---

The Promise

When a person makes a promise of sexual exclusivity with another, it can be argued that it is done with one of the following mindsets:

1. Pure intentions and a genuine commitment to honour the promise.
2. Doubt in their ability to keep the promise.
3. No intention of keeping the promise.

In the latter two cases, the promise made to be monogamous is chosen not out of benefit for their partner but for themselves. In these situations, agreeing to sexual exclusivity is done to either possess the partner or be seen as successful in securing a mate and, therefore, "normal". Immanuel Kant states that morality is based on the motive with which an action is taken and not based upon any perceived benefit that may derive from it.

"To love someone is moral only when love is given free of any expected return, if that love is given simply for the sake of giving love."

Suppose the person making the promise of monogamy does so with the mindset of the latter two scenarios. In that case, they have failed the morality test. The pledge of monogamy has been made because a benefit has been expected, not because they believe they intend to keep it. For these people, taking the vow of sexual exclusivity has put them smack bang in the middle of a moral dilemma. They have chosen to remain loyal to tradition rather than caring for and being fair towards themselves and their partner.

No one can look into the future and predict how one or both of the couple will change, or in that case, how society itself may shift. We can only make promises with the knowledge that we have at the moment. Holding someone to a promise made in a completely different context would suggest a relationship based on dogmatic control, not unconditional love. So herein lies another predicament – understanding that your promise today may only be a prediction for the future.

The Temptation

A desire for another will inevitably arise. Others may contest this notion, which, I would suggest, is either a shining example of the self-deceit described previously or a testament to their skill at suppressing their sexuality. We are human animals with an appreciation for beauty and a thirst for pleasure. And thanks to the separate streams in our brains, we can experience love, lust and attachment for different people.

And yet, for those in monogamous relationships, when feelings for another manifest, they are usually accompanied by a great deal of internal conflict. The person who is attracted to another is then forced to decide between the foundations of liberty and care, demonstrated by being true to their sexuality and sensuality, or the foundations of fairness, loyalty and authority, remaining faithful to their vow of fidelity. Either way, when a desire arises, so does a moral dilemma, and with this, the potential for a great deal of angst. The gravity of this situation is best described in The Myth of Monogamy:

"Whatever our natural inclinations, there is no doubt that human beings are biologically and psychologically capable of having sex with more than one person, often in fairly rapid succession. The evidence is also overwhelming that many people are capable of "making love to" and loving more than one person at the same time. But we are socially prohibited from doing either. This social prohibition is a

powerful one, and in the long run, it generally wins, although usually not without a struggle and often with some short-term defeats. And that struggle – experienced as occasional brief flings for a night or a weekend, long extramarital relationships over months or years, or just fantasised encounters – may be the source of some of the most complex, intense and confusing emotions that human beings experience."[35]

The Admission

What happens if one or both members of the couple act on their desires and commit adultery? Then arrives another weighty dilemma. Do they tell the other that they have been unfaithful? Why is this such a difficult decision to make? I believe it is for two reasons:

We confuse love and sex. As discussed in the previous chapter, with the union of sex and love, any sex outside the couple is seen as an admission of a lack of love. Unless someone uses an affair to sound the death knell for a relationship, they will loathe the idea that their partner believes they no longer love them. And yet, because this belief is ingrained in our psyche, it prevents people from being honest about extra-couple flings or feelings. We don't want the other to think we don't love them, so we choose not to be honest with them. We choose relationship sanctity and security over fairness and compassion.

Fidelity is linked to the ego. Despite all of the declarations of love for another person, if they cheat, then it is common for the aggrieved to throw love out the window and invite hate in. This reaction occurs when the person's sense of self-worth is tied to their partner's ability to remain faithful. If they have sex with someone else, it is not about their partner's needs. It becomes instantly about what the pained party lacks. The focus on "what is wrong with me" and the dominance of ego in the situation prevents the cheater from being treated with any skerrick of consideration. There is no kindness for cheaters because they have broken a promise and exposed their partner's layers of insecurity. Cheaters know that if they are honest, it is likely that they will be made to suffer. It is rare indeed to have the admission of adultery treated with care.

"It is only because of sexuality that we think about truth at all; that we find honesty and kindness at odds with each other."[36]

Given the rate of infidelity and separation in modern relationships, it seems like the odds of each scenario are even. The moral dilemmas of monogamy deliver a 50/50 chance that people will either:

- Cement in their value of monogamy, control their desires and live happily ever after (as long as their partner does the same).
- Prioritise their value of sexual freedom and either cheat or move out of the relationship (or both over a period of time).

It is interesting, isn't it, how the conflict that monogamy presents can either be used to justify staying in a relationship or to end it. The fluctuations between moral priorities may take minutes or months. Still, there will inevitably be movement between the possible preferences of liberty or loyalty. However, the logical approach does not always work. Even if we double down on the moral code of monogamy, feelings of inner conflict can still exist. Even though a mental resolution may be made to exit the relationship and rid oneself of the discomfort, this may not be feasible for many reasons, or the same problems may arise again in the next relationship, continuing the conflict cycle.

Likewise, it is possible that even if one rejects tradition in favour of more authentic arrangements, the moral foundation of authority may still be background noise, whispering accusations of sedition and sacrilege into our subconscious.

Core Concepts

Morals are codes of conduct shaped by society and personal upbringing. They help create stable communities but can also stifle diversity.

Moral dilemmas occur when decisions involve conflicting values. In monogamous relationships, these dilemmas often involve balancing loyalty, fairness, and respect against personal freedom and individual needs.

The expectation of monogamy can create tension by sacrificing personal liberty for relationship stability.

Desire for others is natural and can lead to internal conflict between loyalty and personal freedom.

Admitting infidelity is challenging due to the conflation of sex with love, the feelings of failure involved in not being able to meet society's standards, and the threat it poses to the partner's self-worth.

Monogamy creates ongoing moral tension, forcing individuals to continually choose between fidelity and freedom. This conflict can either justify staying in a relationship or lead to its end, reflecting the inherent struggle between societal expectations and personal desires.

Morals imposed upon a person without the ability to test and shape them to their own personal situation, limits the sense of ownership towards these standards and can create internal conflict and trauma when a person is forced to comply.

Chapter 6 – What's Love Got to Do with It?

The word love is steeped within a vast depth and breadth of individual beliefs and behavioural expectations. The associations we hold around love are shaped by the role models we encountered in our formative years and by every single relationship we have had to date. Therefore, while there may be commonalities in our understanding of love, it is a dangerous assumption to think you know what someone is thinking and feeling when they say, "I love you". Similarly, it is risky to assume that when you say these words to someone else, they will know exactly what is in your mind and heart.

Only when we observe our partner's love in action and experience a misalignment with our expectations do we realise they are not omniscient and cannot immediately and completely discern the intricate details of what we mean by love. Alain de Botton highlights this situation beautifully in his book Essays In Love, where he says:

"Chloe and I could both speak of being in love, and yet this love might mean significantly different things within each of us."[37]

Given the great dependence placed on love then, it seems ridiculous that we spend so little time preventing confusion and clarifying for each other what our associations regarding love are.

This chapter, then, is my attempt to carefully navigate through the labyrinth that is the word love and provide you with food for thought about the role in plays in your intimate relationships.

Defining Love

Psychologists and philosophers alike have come to agree that there are seven different types of love. These are[38]:

1. **Eros**. Sexual or passionate love. Eros is most akin to our notion of romantic love. In Greek mythology, it is a form of madness caused by a hit from Cupid's arrow. Once hit, we "fall in love" and lose all ability to be influenced by reason.

2. **Philia**. Friendship based on mutual benefit, companionship, dependability and trust. Plato believed the best form of friendship arises from and feeds into Eros, being used to transform a lust for possession into a shared understanding of the self, the other and the world.

3. **Storge**. Familial love founded upon familiarity and dependency. This generally pertains to that between parents and their children. However, given enough time, Eros can mature into Storge.

4. **Agape**. Universal love for all people or nature and akin to charity and altruism. It builds a shield to protect against the sinister and provides energy to engage in the world.

5. **Ludus**. Playful and uncommitted interactions, such as teasing, dancing, flirting and seducing. Ludus is all about fun and freedom – no strings attached.

6. **Pragma**. Practical love focused on long-term interests, duty and reason. It prioritises partnership over passion and shared goals over sexual satisfaction.

7. **Philautia**. Self-love. It can be healthy, motivating a person to keep themselves well physically, mentally and spiritually, or harmful, descending into arrogance or narcissism and creating the necessity for a nemesis.

All these types of love play a role in committed adult relationships, with the final one, Philautia, suggested as the central contributor to our success in the other six.

The Flow of Feelings

The other thing to note about these different types of love is that they are largely based on feelings. Yet, feelings are fickle. The word emotion itself suggests that what we are experiencing is "energy in motion"[39], and as such, our feelings will flow and transform like any other energy.

In this way, different forms of love are involved in monogamous relationships over time. A couple may start their journey in Ludus or Eros, pass through Philia and conclude their travels at Storge or Pragma. Pragma is the point for most people where they decide whether they will continue to travel together or decide to part ways in search of the excitement of new Eros or the sport of Ludus. The following diagram shows a general log of one possible journey of love. Plato's ultimate form of friendship is shown here as the dance between Eros and Philia, supported by the duo of attraction and attachment.

Figure 8 - The Journey of Love

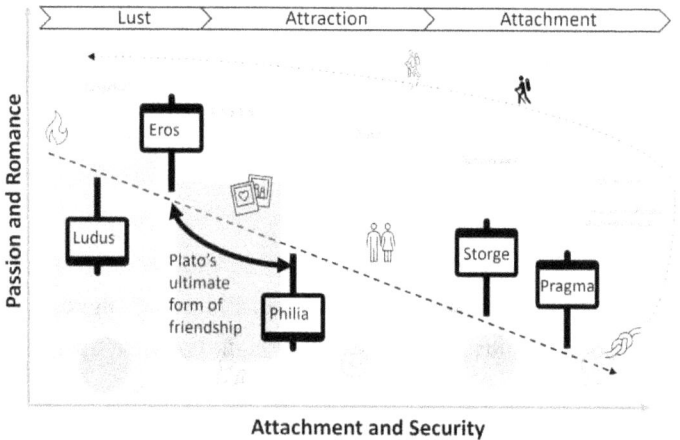

Attachment and Security

It is said that energy never dies. It is merely transformed. And we see this conversion repeatedly in intimate relationships. The initial ecstasy and intoxication of romantic love wanes, usually between 18 months and three years[40]. This is a function of familiarity and desensitisation. In her book *Love and Limerence*, Dorothy Tennov describes this process, stating:

"The ecstasy and obsession decline because the nerve pathways become habituated to the stimulants. They become desensitised to once new feelings."[41]

This view is supported by the psychiatrist Michael Liebowitz who makes it clear that:

"If you want a situation where you and your long-term partner can still get very excited about each other, you will have to work on it because, in some ways, you are bucking a biological tide."[42]

It is a pretty sure bet that the ecstasy of romantic love (Attraction or Eros) will diminish over time. So, the most important question for a monogamous couple then is what this emotion is transformed into. Will it mature into a deep sense of trust and attachment or revolt into more harmful emotions such as apathy, disappointment, anger, bitterness, and hate?

Love In Action

The multitude of influences upon our emotional state makes reliance on love as a feeling incredibly dangerous. The complexity and chaos of our consciousness mean our emotions will ebb and flow, sometimes fast, sometimes slow. Nevertheless, the base emotions we feel at the start of our relationship will not be the same as those felt one year, two years, or twenty years in. Therefore, I propose that instead of defining love by the emotions moving through us, we consider love as the actions we take in response.

This passage from Corinthians is a comprehensive catalogue of what love looks like in action and, interestingly, is a common inclusion in Christian matrimonial sermons:

"Love is patient and kind; love does not envy or boast; it is not arrogant or rude. It does not insist on its own way; it is not irritable or resentful; it does not rejoice at wrongdoing, but rejoices with the truth. Love bears all things, believes all things, hopes all things, endures all things."
-1 Corinthians 13

The selfless, calm and profound nature of love that this verse suggests is motivated by care for us and the other and not just concerned with securing emotional highs. Through actions of faith, kindness and compassion, love aims to reduce the suffering of ourselves and others and help us both move towards happiness. Jim Rohn sums up the nature of love in action beautifully when he says:

"Love is much deeper than a feeling. Love is a commitment we make to people to always treat that person right and honourably."

It is interesting to dig further into one of the Corinthians concepts: love rejoicing with the truth. Sure, truth is a subjective notion, and what a person believes does not have to be founded on facts. But let's suppose you tend to agree with the assertions in this book. In this case, then, the love being lived in a monogamous couple should be strong enough to:

- Celebrate the fact that monogamy is not natural.
- Delight in the fact that we can feel desire and pleasure outside our committed relationships.
- Exult in the fact that we have separate mental functions for lust, romance, and attachment.
- Cheer on the changes in our expressions of love over time.
- Champion open, honest, supportive, and compassionate conversations about individual needs, common goals and how the relationship is meeting them.
- Enjoy the process of understanding ourselves and the other – the good, the bad and the ugly.

Thich Nhat Hahn argues that love and understanding are synonymous and that you cannot truly love someone without appreciating their totality, even the bits that challenge us.

"True love requires deep understanding. In fact, love is another name for understanding. If you do not understand, you cannot love properly. Without understanding, your love will only cause the other person to suffer."[43]

In this way, an open-hearted and authentic desire to understand your partner is an act of love. Judging, blaming, or casting them away because of their humanity indicates that that love is not present.

What Love Is Not

Relationships get jumbled when people use different definitions of love. Here is a list of what some see as love but are actually problematic proxies.

Love is not an emotion

Sure, the way you feel about someone has a huge bearing on how you treat them, but as we have seen, emotions are flippant. At one moment, we can ride the wave of wonder at our partner's intellect. The next, we could feel aggravated by their "smarty pants" antics. And if you believe that love is the ecstasy you feel when riled up in romance, then love will slip away as sure as you can say desensitisation.

Love ≠ sex

Sex can surely be an act of love, but it can also be driven by lust or giddy, transient romance. While sex with someone can consummate and celebrate deep admiration and affection, it can also be a mindless physical release. And while sex can be a transcendental spiritual experience in a safe space, it can also be an impulsive act driven by the pursuit of pleasure.

Love is not a transaction

You don't have to receive love from another to give it. Some people believe they will only give love if they get it from another. Then when the other makes a mistake or behaves in ways that don't meet their expectations, they withdraw and withhold their love. Love becomes a tit-for-tat arrangement. If love is viewed as a transaction, it is only a matter of time before one person does not hold up their end of the bargain, and the game of love is cancelled altogether.

Love is not merging or completion

Many texts espouse the notion that we are all imperfect and that our job is to find our soulmate who will complete us and make us a worthy whole. The view of love as a merging, fusion or completion of the individuals is rooted in insecurity. It suggests that individuals do not consider themselves whole or worthy without the other and are not confident in their personal preferences and opinions.

Love is not dependence

So many of our beliefs about love are reflected in and influenced by modern music. For example:

"I can't live if living is without you." ~ Harry Nilson

"Tear us apart, no, no, no Baby, I would rather be dead." ~ Tina Turner

"I might kill my ex, I still love him, though. Rather be in jail than alone." ~ Sza

When someone loves you, they will do things that are in your best interests, and in this way, you could come to rely upon their assistance and support. However, if you feel that your life is meaningless without them, this is not love – it is dependence. Where there is dependence, there is no equality and no individual freedom, which are cornerstones to love.

Love is not ownership

Again, love songs have a lot to answer for when it comes to polluting our understanding of love.

> *"Still can't believe it when you say you're mine and I am yours" ~ Andy Grammar*

In the early days of romantic love, such assertions can reduce the anxiety that goes along with this relatively unstable and emotional period. However, suppose these claims continue and are believed by the orator. In that case, a dangerous line is crossed into possession and oppression.

Love is not martyrdom

There is a difference between caring for the needs of others and becoming beholden to them. Caring for the needs of others is possible while also caring for yourself. If you become a slave to the needs of others, then if the master leaves, you may end up a bitter wreck, wondering why you wasted so many years of your life, sacrificing yourself for others.

> *"All love that has not caused the freedom of spirit, easily turns into hatred." ~ Benedictus de Spinoza*

Love is not security

Love does not mean that the other person will be with you for the rest of your life. Love also does not mean that the type of relationship you have today is the same one you will have tomorrow or ten years from now. Love does not secure a lifestyle or preserve a point-in-time experience of happiness. What true love does assure, though, is that whether you remain with the other or not, they will have your best interests at heart and treat you with patience and kindness.

"The search for security is undertaken by the weakest part of the personality, by fear, inadequacy, fatigue and anxiety."[44]

Love is not time-bound

Remember, love endures all things, including time.

A true love for someone, an honest desire to see them flourish, exists across time and relationships. In this way, with unconditional love, you can still want the best for the other person, even if it means that to maintain your wellbeing, you are no longer in their life. It is also easy to imagine that in unconditional love, you can be happy for your current partner if they find happiness with another.

"Lovers end, love continues." ~ Osho

Love is not fear

As a person who has recently shunned organised religion, I can't believe I am quoting the Bible again, but the point is pertinent.

"There is no fear in love, but perfect love casts out fear. For fear has to do with punishment, and whoever fears has not been perfected in love". ~ 1 John 4:18

So many of the misguided notions of love are grounded in fear. Exchange, merging, completion, dependence, ownership, and martyrdom are all behaviours driven by fears of not getting enough, not being enough, and being alone.

Love ≠ Monogamy (and vice versa)

We have seen that the actions of love may or may not be associated with monogamy. That is, love and monogamy do not have to co-exist[45]. They may collide when a couple decides that a sexually exclusive relationship is important to them both. Through patience, care, openness and understanding, they support each on this path. However, love can also exist where there is what traditionalists would see as "infidelity" by one or both partners. Love is present in this relationship, too, where there is awareness, understanding, empathy and honesty. Love, then, is neither a prerequisite nor a product of monogamy. I would argue, though, that it is essential for a flourishing monogamous union.

Core Concepts

Our understanding of love is deeply personal and shaped by a lifetime of individual experiences.

There are seven types of love: Eros (passionate), Philia (friendship), Storge (familial), Agape (universal), Ludus (playful), Pragma (practical), and Philautia (self-love).

All these forms can play roles in relationships, but self-love (Philautia) is key to nurturing the other types.

The journey of love often evolves through different stages, such as moving from Eros to Pragma, influenced by time and familiarity.

Emotions are fluid and can change over time, making love as an emotion unreliable. Love is best seen in actions rather than just emotions.

Love is not just an emotion, sex, a transaction, or ownership. It is not about merging, dependence, martyrdom, security, or bound by time. It transcends fear and is about understanding and genuinely caring for another's wellbeing.

Love does not necessarily equate to monogamy, nor does monogamy guarantee love. Love can exist in both monogamous and non-monogamous relationships.

Love does not depend on the relationship form but on the level of awareness, understanding and honesty held within the couple.

Chapter 7 – What's Maturity Got to Do with It?

As we have heard in the previous chapter, confluent love requires partners to overcome their fears and be willing to reveal their own needs and concerns. Each person must be brave enough to be vulnerable and confident enough to allow their partner to do the same. True love then takes great courage. Dr Gordon Neufeld would suggest that relationships based on love also see the individuals within them operating in growth mode.

"Down to the very cellular level, human beings are either in defensive mode or growth mode, but they cannot be in both at the same time."[46]

This resonates with the idea that a person can be driven by either fear or love, not both simultaneously. Fear shuts us down, fostering defensiveness and dishonesty, whereas love is open and accepting, enabling individual and relational growth. For love to flourish, both partners need the courage to be vulnerable and allow space for each other to grow.

Reaching a "growth mode" is no small feat; it involves moving through stages of self-discovery and maturity. It takes time and experience to truly understand who we are, break away from societal pressures, and present our full, authentic selves to others. This journey is essential for creating a fulfilling monogamous relationship, one in which both individuals bring maturity and self-acceptance.

Maturity in Stages: Dr. Kegan's Theory of Adult Development

Dr. Robert Kegan's Theory of Adult Development outlines five stages of maturity, with the latter stages particularly relevant for building a healthy relationship. These stages range from the Imperial Mind, focused on personal needs, to the Self-Transforming Mind, where individuals fully embrace growth and transformation. Each stage reflects a different level of self-awareness and relationship to others, shaping how individuals approach intimate relationships, including monogamy.

According to Dr Kegan, there are five stages of The Theory of Adult Development[47] which are summarised in the table on the following page. The stages of development highlight how maturity can influence relationship choices, particularly in monogamy. Those at earlier stages may view relationships as a source of validation or personal gain, while those in later stages prioritize mutual growth and authenticity.

Dr. Robert Kegan's Theory of Adult Development			
Stage	Stage Name	Characteristics	% of adult pop.
Stage 1	Impulsive Mind		early childhood
Stage 2	Imperial Mind	• It's all about my needs • I will follow norms and trends to get rewards and avoid punishment	adolescence, 6% of the adult population
Stage 3	Socialised Mind	• It's all about what you think of me • I seek out and depend upon external validation. • I am defined by others.	58% of the adult population
Stage 4	Self-Authoring Mind	• It's all about what I think of myself. • I take responsibility for my own opinions and actions. • I have the power to create the life that I want.	35% of the adult population
Stage 5	Self-Transforming Mind	• I release myself from expectations around my identity. • I am free to question, challenge, expand and reinvent myself.	1% of the adult population

The Imperial Mind: It's All About Me

The Imperial Mind, typically found in adolescence but present in about six percent of adults, is self-centred and driven by personal needs. Individuals at this stage see relationships transactionally, basing decisions on the personal benefits they gain. In monogamy, they may commit to exclusivity for security or social approval, not out of genuine connection. This stage is marked by an external focus: adhering to societal norms or rebelling against them based on what yields the most benefit.

The Socialized Mind: It's All About What You Think of Me

Most adults—about 58%—operate from the Socialized Mind, where self-worth is deeply intertwined with external validation. In this stage, individuals are defined by their relationships and the views of others. They often pursue monogamy to fit in, satisfy family expectations, or fulfill cultural norms rather than for personal fulfillment.

Alain de Botton describes this dependence on relationships for identity: "Without love, we lose the ability to possess a proper identity; within love, there is a constant confirmation of ourselves." For those at this stage, love is necessary to affirm their worth, making relationships crucial for their sense of self. However, there are risks in depending so heavily on external validation. This stage often involves repressing vulnerabilities and adapting to the expectations of others. Individuals may withhold parts of themselves, fearing rejection or judgment, which undermines true intimacy and self-expression.

Social media plays a role in reinforcing the Socialized Mind, as it amplifies conformity and discourages deviation from trends. By sharing curated versions of ourselves, we become trapped in a cycle of comparison, constantly seeking affirmation and validation. This dependence on external validation can hinder genuine connection in monogamous relationships, as individuals are often more focused on meeting societal expectations than fostering a meaningful partnership.

Despite these challenges, the Socialized Mind is an essential developmental stage. It helps individuals understand the importance of connection and community, which is a necessary foundation for later stages of maturity. However, those who remain stuck in this mindset may find themselves struggling in relationships, continually seeking validation rather than nurturing individuality and growth.

The Self-Authoring Mind: It's All About What I Think of Myself

Transitioning to the Self-Authoring Mind requires courage and self-reflection. At this stage, individuals begin to define their identity based on personal values rather than societal expectations. They take responsibility for their actions and make relationship choices based on what they believe is right for themselves, not to fit in or please others. This shift allows for a deeper sense of independence, enabling individuals to contribute to a relationship without losing their identity.

In intimate relationships, the Self-Authoring Mind brings freedom from the need for external validation. People at this stage prioritize authentic connections and embrace differences rather than seeking to merge identities. This perspective fosters a balanced and respectful partnership, where both individuals can grow and flourish.

A.H. Maslow, in his work on motivation and personality, highlights the maturity that allows individuals to accept their inherent dichotomies—such as the need for both independence and connection. The Self-Authoring Mind provides a framework for navigating these opposing needs within a relationship, fostering understanding, compassion, and constructive dialogue.

The Self-Transforming Mind: Beyond Identity

At the Self-Transforming Mind, individuals move beyond conventional self-definitions, embracing fluidity and complexity. They no longer feel constrained by social labels or rigid identities. This stage allows them to see relationships as dynamic, evolving connections rather than fixed roles. In monogamy, such individuals may no longer feel the need to label their relationship or restrict themselves to societal definitions of love. Instead, they prioritize growth and support their partner's evolution as well.

David Whyte describes this stage as one of expansive, fluid maturity: "Maturity beckons, asking us to be larger, more fluid, more elemental; a story...just, astonishingly, about to occur." This mindset fosters deep connection without the pressure of conformity, allowing individuals to engage fully with the present moment and embrace change.

Germaine Greer also suggests that mature individuals may not feel confined by monogamy, as they have developed a self-assuredness that allows for loving openly without fear. However, the success of any relationship model, monogamous or otherwise, depends on the maturity level of each person involved.

Maturity is Not Defined by Age

Maturity does not necessarily correlate with age. While many people progress through Kegan's stages over time, others may remain in earlier stages well into adulthood. It's not uncommon to find individuals in midlife re-evaluating their relationships, seeking greater authenticity, and questioning traditional views on monogamy. Life experiences, rather than age, often drive these reflections, leading individuals to explore new facets of themselves.

This questioning of traditional monogamy is common among those who feel restricted by societal norms or who desire a deeper sense of individuality within their relationships. As people mature, they may feel a stronger pull toward autonomy and self-expression, prompting them to reassess the dynamics of their intimate relationships.

Mature vs. Immature Love

In relationships, maturity influences the quality of love. Alain de Botton differentiates between "mature love" and "immature love." Mature love involves accepting both the good and bad within ourselves and others. It is calm, grounded, and free from obsession. This love allows for a friendship that is deepened by sexual connection and mutual respect. In contrast, immature love swings between idealization and disappointment, marked by intense highs and lows and an unstable sense of fulfillment.

This concept aligns with the Hermetic Law of Correspondence—what we bring into a relationship affects what we get out of it. Entering a relationship from a place of love and self-assurance leads to a balanced and fulfilling partnership, whereas fear-based relationships often result in conflict and disappointment. As the saying goes, "Garbage in, garbage out." The quality of one's inner life reflects in the quality of one's relationships.

Maturity as an Input to Successful Monogamy

Creating a fulfilling, loving relationship requires courage, self-awareness, and a commitment to growth. For a relationship to thrive, both partners must bring maturity, self-acceptance, and authenticity to the union. As Dr. Kegan's Theory of Adult Development illustrates, the higher stages of maturity—the Self-Authoring and Self-Transforming Minds—allow individuals to contribute to a relationship from a place of independence and genuine connection.

At its core, true love requires individuals to move beyond societal expectations and find value in their authentic selves. It challenges them to build relationships that honour both individuality and partnership. As Alain de Botton describes, mature love embraces complexity, balance, and understanding, whereas immature love is often mired in insecurity and idealization.

In the end, love that is rooted in maturity and self-awareness brings not only fulfillment but also resilience. Such a love allows individuals to grow both within the relationship and independently, creating a foundation for lasting happiness and mutual respect.

Core Concepts

Love flourishes when both individuals are in "growth mode."

The stage of adult development influences how individuals approach monogamy and relationships.

When people are operating from the socialised mind, they seek validation through relationships, conforming to social norms to affirm self-worth.

Higher maturity stages bring independence and the ability to embrace individuality in relationships. Self-aware partners can balance personal growth with relational harmony.

Mature love is rooted in acceptance, balance, and mutual respect, while immature love fluctuates between idealization and disappointment, often driven by insecurity and unmet needs.

Successful monogamy relies on maturity, self-acceptance, and authenticity. Love rooted in growth and self-awareness builds resilience, allowing for individual development within the relationship.

Chapter 8 – What's Disney Got to Do with It?

It may seem unexpected to delve into the world of Disney in a book about adult relationships. However, it's crucial to understand that our beliefs about intimate relationships and our expectations of monogamy and marriage were significantly shaped during our formative years. Until the age of eight, a child is like a sponge, absorbing information about how the world works. What they are exposed to during this time becomes a platform for their future beliefs.

Given Disney's prominent position in family entertainment, it's likely that our adult relationships have been influenced by the cartoon characters we watched as children. Disney princess films, in particular, are rich in relationship role models. Therefore, Disney has played a pivotal role in defining the characteristics we believe make for a successful monogamous relationship.

Ironically, the magic woven into these children's films is the stage upon which a host of adult disappointments are set. Because wedged firmly within the naivety and charm is an unrealistic set of expectations about intimate relationships. Over and over again, the child is presented with the promise of one true love, the assurance of love at first sight and the possibility of a happily ever after. These films tell us that entering a monogamous relationship (generally marriage) is a magical endgame. Through this, we will become whole and worthy.

One might assume that as we mature, we would outgrow these idealistic notions of love and gain a more realistic understanding of relationships. However, research has shown that while most adults recognise the themes in Disney films as unrealistic, they still hold onto them. Moreover, many adults believe that these fantasy endings are possible for them, and that one day, their prince (or princess or non-binary royal heir) will arrive to sweep them off their feet[48]. So, while our logical, adult brains know fairy tales are a fiction, our inner child, full of imagination and innocence, still yearns for them to become a reality.

Ultimately, our beliefs become our reality. So, if the majority of adults still have faith in fairy tales, then it is inevitable that many of us will spend our lives trying to mimic the monogamous role models we grew up with on screen.

There are five main deceptions embedded in Disney movies that, if crammed into our core beliefs, expose us to a future full of bitterness and disappointment. These themes become subliminal indicators of relationship success through repetition.

1. Love = romance
2. Love happens at first sight
3. There is one true love
4. My partner will fix my problems
5. We will live happily ever after.

Love = Romance

Romantic love, or Eros, characterises the early stage of an intimate relationship and is imbued with extreme emotions. It is known for its experiences of ecstasy. There are heady highs when lovers' eyes lock and thrill from the subtlest touch. This state of romantic bliss is depicted delightfully in Disney films. When the happy hormones have kicked in for our animated friends, they sing with baby birds and dance around in the dust.

However, romance is also a time of great anxiety. The couple is still uncertain about each other and their future, so it is mired in trepidation and flooded with the fear of losing their ultimate source of happiness. We also see the sheer desperation of romantic love in Disney films. Cinderella's prince calls forth his army to find his one true love. And Ariel thinks nothing of giving up her voice to be a part of her prince's world. In the films, the turbulence and tension of the conflicting emotions are resolved through marriage. The couple is joined as one forever more, secure in the bonds of monogamy and matrimony. With this union, the raptures of romance become sanctified, and all worries are washed away with the first wedding toast.

The association ingrained through the Disney films then is that romance equals love. However, as the research shows, the romantic period is programmed biologically only to last around three to five years[49]. When romance wanes, does this mean love has been lost? If we no longer feel passion, excitement, and a fear of loss, then does it mean that there is no more love? When desire dies, is this the sign that the couple has fallen out of love?

While innately, we may understand that there are many expressions of love available on the market, if we have purchased the one sold by Disney, then after a few years, when the shine rubs off, you may wonder if you could trade love in for a newer model. Preferably one with lots of bells and whistles and a wish-granting genie! Because, given time, the Disney model of love you have purchased may no longer work. It has stopped delivering what you had been promised on purchase, being a happily ever after.

Love At First Sight

The three most well-known Disney princesses, Snow White, Cinderella and Sleeping Beauty, met their princes one day and married them the next. For Snow White, all it took for love to blossom was a glance and a shared song. And a look was all it took for Ariel to be lovestruck. A mere dance convinced Cinderella and Aurora that they had found their destiny.

Disney films target children, so the storylines must be simple. They must also reach their conclusion quickly to cater to the audience's limited attention span. However, let's get real. There is no way you can know a person after just one dance. Moreover, one could suggest that you can never fully know a person. In many ways, we may never completely understand ourselves. So many of our motivations and behaviours are subconscious and driven by innate fears and desires. You need to be a mind-reader to know in just one dance whether you share the values that can sustain a lifetime together. This reality is cleverly construed in the film Frozen, and through Anna's doomed relationship with the sly and suave Hans. When Hans refuses to share what everyone believes will be true love's kiss, thus sentencing Anna to death, he exposes the crafty way he has duped his darling. Anna's reliance on love at first sight meant she missed some very sinister signs.

If we are to be truthful, what we are witnessing on the screen is lust at first sight. The protagonists are all the most beautiful specimens in the land. They are all of child-bearing age and are deemed desirable by every available suitor. Perhaps then, just like these films confuse the notions of love and romance, they also confuse the states of lust and love. One of the truest tests of love comes when the couple is under the greatest of pressures and when one or both are at their very worst. Love depends upon the exchange of emotions, not only pleasant but also painful ones. For this reason, Disney films cross the line from being simply innocent (or ignorant) to dangerously deceptive.

My One True Love

Despite the ballrooms full of potential partners, the events unfolding in the Disney films reveal there can only be one true love for each prince or princess. Only one person across the entire community can be the keeper of true love's kiss, and only one can be trusted with the Princess' heart, frailty and future.

The implications of this notion are dire. The idea that there is one true love can be used to chicken out on critical conversations that may help a relationship and its individuals grow. The logic goes like this - if there is just one person who can satisfy your needs, and if the person you are with is no longer satisfying your needs, then the obvious conclusion is that they are not the one – they are not my one true love. It is not a big leap from dissatisfaction to believing you have made a mistake in choosing your partner. You have been duped. Your partner is not the prince (or princess) you were looking for, so now you are both liberated and justified to abscond and search for your real true love.

However, as we have seen in the discussion around human neurology, we are actually wired to be able to love more than one person at a time. Of course, Disney films were bound to present the morals of the day, which were, and still are, dominated by the gold standard of monogamy. So, the one true love theme is understandable. However, a subtext to this theme cuts deeper than intimacy and into self-identity. The idea that there is one other person in the world who is meant for you implies that alone, you are incomplete. Finding and possessing your true love makes you whole and worthy. Those who have not yet found their one true love remain lesser humans.

My Partner Will Fix My Problems

The idea of being rescued by another brings up another precarious theme in Disney films – that the entry of your one true love makes all of your troubles disappear. For Snow White and Aurora, the presence of their princes heralded escape from the curse of endless slumber. The prince was also there to rescue Cinderella from the claws of the evil stepmother and the bonds of servitude. For Ariel, Prince Eric delivered liberation from boredom at the bottom of the ocean and ceaseless conversations with crayfish. In Disney films, it is not just damsels that rely on another to be saved from distress. The Beast needed someone to love him so he could be freed from the curse that caused him to be hideous, ostracised and isolated.

The subliminal message here is that the one you love should be able to take away all of your problems and even save you from yourself. It is as if having a partner reduces your personal responsibility for dealing with the duplicity of life, creating a life you love and becoming a better person. The yearning for things to be easy is a normal part of human nature, so it should be no surprise when the desire to be rescued shows up. Nevertheless, projecting this onto our partners and having them take responsibility for our future happiness is disrespectful.

Because what happens after several years with your prince or princess if you are still poor, angry, unfit, lonely, hating your job and are no closer to having your dreams come true? If you buy into this Disney theme, then you may begin to believe that this person you have chosen is not the one that can help you lift the curse – they are not noble, dignified or clever enough, or even worse, their love is not strong enough to counteract the toxicity of past trauma. It is easier to go searching for someone who will make us happy than to put effort into doing this for ourselves.

We tend to forget that the only constant in any relationship is ourselves. Therefore, a happily ever after depends just as much on us as on our intimate other.

Happily Ever After

The fundamental principle of monogamy is that the couple is bound together for life. It is nowhere shown more clearly than the traditional marriage vow of "till death do we part." Even the legislative definition of marriage dictates that it is a union "voluntarily entered into for life." However, the ability for divorce makes nonsense of this promise, as the couple knows there is always an out. While the life sentence is a commitment made on one day, the couple will not be held to it by anything other than their own conscience.

I want to think that those entering a monogamous relationship do so with the honest intention of holding true to their promise and doing all they can to create a happily ever after. But how many couples do you know that have a merry marriage? I may be travelling in the wrong circles, but all I see are partnerships at various stages of detachment, deceit, disillusionment, and despair.

Were they realistically expecting a happily ever after? Did they believe that their union would grant the wish of eternal bliss? The research suggests that the answer is yes[50]. Even as adults, we still buy into this possibility and end up bitter and disappointed when our expectations are revealed to be nothing short of naïve.

However, one aspect of this theme is rarely explored, and that is the definition of happiness. The happiness portrayed in Disney films is hedonistic, defined as the pleasure gained from external sources. Acknowledgement, awards, material possessions, displays of affection, and attestations of love are all things that bring the characters happiness. However, all of these sources are superficial and short-lived. As we have seen with the nature of romance, they are transitory.

There is another conception of happiness called eudemonia. Eudemonia is the happiness of achieving personal fulfilment and progressing towards one's full potential. If this is the happiness sought in a relationship, then the expectations of our partners are very different. Instead of status, security, sex or self-esteem, the partner is seen as an aid to becoming your best self. In eudemonic happiness, happily ever after is not an eternity of ecstasy but more like a mundane commitment to help each other grow and flourish. Nevertheless, there is magic in the mundane. In this case, it is the breathtaking process of watching another person becoming all they can be and passing from this life with no regrets.

Both hedonistic and eudemonic happiness is essential. We all need and seek pleasure in our lives. However, to only measure the success of our relationships by the gauge of hedonistic happiness is short-sighted. In monogamous relationships, the pleasure we gain from our loved ones will inevitably fade. This outcome is a function of both familiarity and biology. But what if, instead of clinging to such a simplistic and superficial view, we were able to consider the relationship as a medium through which each person can also achieve eudemonia?

In theory, this may mean we witness our partners grow and evolve each day and transition and transform into their true selves with each passing year. There is no room for stagnation or boredom in this model but the continual celebration of the resilience and potential of the people we love. The relationship ceases to become a burden and a process by which each person shrinks into the other. Instead, it becomes an adventure and a mechanism for exploring and expanding what is possible. I would love to see this kind of relationship immortalised in film.

Core Concepts

Our beliefs about relationships and monogamy are significantly influenced by Disney films we watched as children.

Disney films promote five key misconceptions:

1. **Love = Romance:** Romance naturally fades over time, causing confusion about the true nature of enduring love.
2. **Love at First Sight**: True understanding and deep connection take time and effort, not just a glance or dance.
3. **One True Love:** This can lead to unrealistic standards, making people abandon relationships when their partner doesn't meet every need.
4. **My Partner Will Fix My Problems**: This undermines personal responsibility and creates unrealistic expectations of relationships.
5. **Happily Ever After**: This view overlooks the reality of relationship challenges and the need for personal growth and effort from both partners.

Disney's portrayal of happiness focuses on hedonistic joy from external sources, whereas a healthier, more sustainable approach to happiness in relationships would be eudemonic—finding fulfilment and personal growth.

Research shows that while most adults recognise the themes in Disney films as unrealistic, they still believe that these fantasy endings are possible for them.

Chapter 9 – What's God Got to Do with It?

If you describe yourself as an agnostic or an atheist, you may wish to skip this chapter. However, you would be incorrect in assuming that because you have rejected religion, it has no relevance to your intimate relationships. Marriage, sex, adultery and love are all topics covered in the holy books of the world's major religions and have been the most significant influence on modern morality. In Western nations, our laws and social norms around monogamy and sexuality more broadly are directly descended from the relationship role model of Adam and Eve. Whether you like it or not, your beliefs and behaviours in coupledom have been shaped by what we have been told are the righteous rules of God.

What is interesting, though, is that while humanity has invested enormous effort in replacing the myth of Eden with the science of evolution, we have not applied the same rigour to determining how 'right' the righteous relationship arrangements are.

The purpose of this chapter is to reflect on what we are told God expects from our adult relationships and whether these calm or compound the dilemmas that monogamy presents. It is delivered with the proviso that just as I am not a psychoanalyst or anthropologist, I am also neither a theologian nor a biblical scholar. My views are informed only by my personal experience of being raised and educated in Catholic institutions and my superficial understanding of religious doctrines. In this chapter, I will only address Christianity, given that it is the sole religion I have been intimately exposed to. I would hate to insult those of other faiths with my ignorance.

How Do We Know God?

Before we dive into the relevant doctrines, I would like to take some time to review how we have come to know God's instructions concerning intimate relationships. Through what source have we come to know God's wishes? Ultimately, we have come to know God through the prophets. These prophets told their people that God had spoken to them, and their people believed them. A prophet, then, is a person who has enough political clout to be held credible. Many more people may also have discussions with divinities but, without suitable sponsorship, are merely deemed to be deranged. It seems there is a fine line between being a prophet and a psycho, with the first wielding much power and the second most likely to be punished in some form.

These prophets, the ensuing disciples, and scribes were all men who lived thousands of years ago in lands far from our own. The Torah and books of the Bible were written between 1500 BC and 95 AD, and the scriptures span various cultural contexts.

What would have been common across them all, though, is that they were written in a time and place when men were seen as superior and where the patriarchy wielded power. Marriages were not a product of love but a pragmatic arrangement to unite families and share resources. Likely, marriages would have been arranged by the fathers, with women transitioning from a possession of the Father to then being owned by the husband. Unsurprisingly, one of the first things we are told is that man was made in God's likeness, so obviously, God is a man. This depiction would have been appropriate for the time and place in which the scriptures were written.

Yet, if we believe what we read in the Old Testament, it becomes clear that God is often depicted as a grumpy old man. He is described as having a penchant for wrath, especially when other deities are involved. This portrayal of God as violent and vengeful, known for smiting, slaying, and sending pestilence to punish his enemies, raises questions about the nature of the relationship between fear and love. We are told to fear God, yet there can be no love where there is fear. This interpretation of God's character in the Old Testament is one that I find troubling and worthy of further exploration.

This may be why Jesus was sent. We are told that Jesus was love personified. He preached compassion, selflessness, humility, and care for the less fortunate. It appears that Jesus was sent to clean up God's merciless mess and put a relatable face on a religion previously founded on fear. Jesus was the caring balance to his Father's fearsomeness and presented a tangible transition in religious tenets towards tenderness.

One commonality between God and Jesus, though, is pertinent. Neither of these deities wrote anything themselves. We have no texts attributed to the Almighty and no notes jotted down by Jesus himself. We rely fully on other people's descriptions of what they believed was important for a good life. In this way, faith plays a huge role in religion to bring hope for an eternity in heaven and discourage doubt in the dogma. We are told to believe in the teachings of the Bible even though we have no personal connection to the authors and no ability to validate the stories told. We must have faith that the prophets' doctrines represent God's will and the right way to live to secure our eternal happiness.

A more important point is whether we can truly know God at all. We understand he is:

"Perfect in power, wisdom, and goodness".[51]

Still, this level of enlightenment and excellence is beyond our mortal comprehension. If God exists as described in the Bible, we would have only witnessed a microscopic view of his power. There is no way that any language or literary form can accurately portray the limitless and luminous existence of a divine being. We can only ever view it through our frail human form and incomplete intelligence.

What Did God And Jesus Do?

Given these limitations, what messages can be construed from the Bible as to what makes for a righteous relationship?

The Ten Commandments are among the most famous teachings on the behaviours that please God. They are instructions handed by God to Moses on two stone tablets and became the backbone of Judaism and later Christianity. The Commandments have two rules when it comes to sexual relationships. These are:

4. Though shalt not commit adultery.

5. Though shalt not covet thy neighbour's house, thy neighbour's wife or his slaves, or his animals, or anything of thy neighbour.

The first commandment is pretty clear – do not have sex with anyone else outside of marriage. Note that this applies to both men and women. The second reflects the role of wives as possessions and (very kindly) affords them the same consideration as slaves and donkeys – not to be desired. The role of these rules was to prevent anyone from acting out on their envy and disrupting the concord that marriages created in the community. They were intended to remind people that there was something more important than their selfish yearnings: society's integrity, peace and stability.

What is not often discussed, though, is that there appears to be an acknowledgement that the stipulation of sexual exclusivity is not always easy to follow. For example, in the Old Testament, we are told Sarah could not bear children and asked her husband, Abraham, to have sex with his slave Hagar to build a family (Genesis 16). In this case, procreation took precedence over fidelity. God did not disdain this act and, in fact, appeared to condone it. He sent angels to protect Hagar and her son Ishmael from the wrath of Sarah when her previously judicious act turned to jealousy.

Jesus followed in his Father's footsteps, protecting and pardoning women taken in adultery. In doing so, he allegedly uttered the famous words:

"Let he who is without sin cast the first stone."

These simple words hold enormous significance. With this statement, Jesus made it clear that, yes, in the Christian religion, adultery is a sin. But more importantly, we are all guilty of some sin and potentially of the same one that led the adulterous woman before him to be punished. He recognised the societal value of monogamy was important. However, at the same time, he also recognised the complexity of the human condition and that sexual desire was innate and inevitable.

Additionally, while others saw prostitutes as the devil's handmaidens, dragging men into the den of earthly desire, Jesus saw them as mere humans like the rest of us. He did not push them away, repelled by their lowly status, but allowed them to wash his feet and praised them for their honesty and humility. He had more regard for prostitutes who were open and sincere about their predicament than he did for the priests who tarnished the temple with commercialist corruption.

There is another commandment we still need to cover that must also be considered. That is number nine:

"Thou shalt not bear false witness against thy neighbour."

When it comes to intimate relationships, this commandment is just as important as the explicit banning of adultery, because it acknowledges that through our lack of honesty with ourselves, and our partner, we may also cause a great deal of hurt. It suggests that partners must be honest about:

- Their willingness to be or remain monogamous.
- Any deviance from the vow of fidelity in a monogamous union.

This first requires a high level of self-awareness and self-sincerity before we can share our truth with others. Certainly, Jesus appeared to commend courage, open-heartedness, and authenticity more than he celebrated blind compliance with the commandments.

These examples clarify that Jesus placed primacy on the moral foundation of care over the more rigid rules-based foundation of authority. These actions indicate that honesty, kindness and regard for the individual spirit were more important than the strict application of rules and religious dogmas. Love was more important than the law. Jesus could see how being human brings so many competing desires and disturbing dualities. His response was not to strangle people with strictures but to use compassion to bring understanding, reconciliation and peace.

How Sex Became Bad

Over the centuries after his death, though, the benevolence shown by Jesus to the sexual nature of humanity was replaced with the raging insecurity of the church forefathers. Desire and sexual pleasure were believed to bring out the worst in people, so they required censorship and tight boundaries to maintain safe communities and communion with their deities. Through this approach, they unwittingly indicated their understanding of the sometimes-distressing nature of human desires. However, instead of considering the Jesus route, they chose the path of suppression.

This view is best reflected in the writings of Paul the Apostle. In 1 Corinthians (1-7), he states:

"It is good for a man not to have sexual relations with a woman. But because of the temptation to sexual immorality, each man should have his own wife and each woman her own husband. The husband should give to his wife her conjugal rights, and likewise the wife to her husband. For the wife does not have authority over her own body, but the husband does. Likewise the husband does not have authority over his own body, but the wife does. Do not deprive one another, except perhaps by agreement for a limited time, that you may devote yourselves to prayer; but then come together again, so that Satan may not tempt you because of your lack of self-control."

In this way, monogamy has been enforced as it is seen as essential to save humanity from our inherent lack of sexual self-restraint. Thanks to Adam and Eve, we are seen as inherently sinful creatures who cannot be trusted with our sexuality. Our instincts must be curbed and constrained for the convenience of the community and the peace of the powers that rule it.

While Jesus had compassion for our human frailty, the fathers of the church that followed appeared to be far less flexible. The liberty and care approach presented by the Son of God became mangled through the corridors of power and transformed into archaic dogma and dominance. As with any organisation, the larger it gets, the more formalisation is required to maintain order. In this way, individuality became secondary to the rules of the institution and the preservation of its power.

In this way, religion has been used to instigate righteousness, a dogmatic view of right and wrong. It creates strict moral guidelines that are used not only to enforce what is believed to be the will of God but also to prevent contamination by corrupt idols, the dilution of identity or the confusion of the community. While Jesus' actions attest to his desire to unite people through understanding and compassion, religion has created a morality that divides people through differences.

The Golden Rule

Yet, as proposed by John Stuart Mill, religion (viewed as a collection of morals) can be used to stimulate conversations about what we would like to have in common, which creates the potential for broader, more inclusive communities[52]. From a purely practical perspective, focusing on common beliefs would also allow us to hedge our bets. If we were wrong and the other God is 'it', then at least we would have fulfilled some of their rules and had a chance at an attractive afterlife.

And the exciting thing is this is possible. Because across every religion, there is one common commandment called The Golden Rule:

"Do not do to others what you would not have done to you."

This single teaching is expressed across the vast variety of creeds and cultures as follows:

'Whatever you wish that men would do to you, do so to them. This is the meaning of the Law of Moses and the teaching of the Prophets.'—Christianity, The Bible, Matthew 7:12

'What is hateful to you, do not do to your neighbour; that is the whole Torah; all the rest of it is commentary.'—Judaism, Talmud, Shabbat 31a

'Not one of you is a believer until he loves for his brother what he loves for himself.'—Islam, Hadith of an-Nawawi 13

'Never impose on others what you would not choose for yourself.'—Confucianism, Analects, XV.24

'Regard your neighbour's gain as your gain, and your neighbour's loss as your loss.'—Taoism, T'ai Shang Kan Ying P'ien.

'For a state that is not pleasant or delightful to me must also be to him; and a state that is not pleasing or delightful to me, how could I inflict that upon another?'—Buddhism, Samyutta Nikaya v.353

'That nature alone is good which refrains from doing to another whatsoever is not good for itself.'—Zoroastrianism, Dadisten-i-dinik, 94.5

'Lay not on any soul a load that you would not wish to be laid upon you, and desire not for anyone the things that you would not desire for yourself.'— Baha'i, Baha'u'llah Gleanings

'This is the s um of duty: do not do to others what would cause pain if done to you.' —Hinduism, Mahabharata 5c1517

'One should treat all creatures in the world as one would like to be treated.'— Jainism, Mahavira, Sutrakiritanga

The Golden Rule is a crucial and clarifying perspective on what God, any or all gods, want for our intimate relationships. There is a cacophony around what is right and just concerning sexual unions. And yet, none of the commentary or criticism has enabled us to reduce the rate of adultery and divorce and the trauma that follows it. Certainly, strict tenets of faith are becoming less relevant as people unsubscribe to organised religions and the cancel culture runs rampant on the commandments. Then, perhaps what is most important is to get back to the core, the heart of what being a good person means. After all, isn't that where all religions began – as a way to guide people to live a good life?

Core Concepts

Religious beliefs have shaped societal norms around marriage, sex, adultery, and love.

Our understanding of God's expectations in relationships comes from ancient texts and prophets, mostly men from patriarchal societies.

The Ten Commandments, especially those prohibiting adultery and coveting another's spouse, underscore monogamy's societal role in maintaining stability.

The Bible offers mixed messages: while God's commandments enforce sexual exclusivity, stories like that of Abraham and Hagar show flexibility when procreation is prioritised.

Jesus' approach valued care, liberty, and honesty suggesting that understanding and kindness were more important than rigid rules.

Over time, religious institutions shifted from Jesus' compassionate stance to strict control over human sexuality.

Monogamy became a tool for curbing human sexuality which was seen as sinful and a threat to social stability.

Despite differing doctrines, a common thread across religions is The Golden Rule: "Do not do to others what you would not have done to you." This principle emphasizes mutual respect and kindness in relationships, transcending specific religious mandates.

Chapter 10 – What's The Law Got to Do with It?

It could be argued that the laws of any land signify what is truly important for the peace and prosperity of its people. However, while those deciding the laws are usually elected representatives, they do not necessarily represent the diversity of the population. It is also fair to say that the cumbersome and protracted process of law-making results in regulations that are no longer relevant.

The more troubling case is when laws not only fail to resolve but actually create moral conflicts. This is a pressing issue, as legislation can sow confusion in the minds of the citizens about what is truly important. Two cases are particularly relevant to our modern, intimate relationships.

1. The Australian Sex Discrimination Act (1984) prohibits discrimination against people based on sex, sexual orientation, gender identity, intersex status, and marital or relationship status. This Act makes it clear a person should be able to live as bi-sexual or polyamorous without impediment. However, under the Marriage Act (1961), a person can only be married to one other or risk being charged under the laws of bigamy and potentially imprisoned for five years. Does it appear then that the federal government is discriminating against people in terms of both sexual orientation and relationship status? This situation suggests that people are free to live lives true to their own sexuality and relationship values. However, they will not be supported to formalise any relationship unless it is a monogamous union. So, in the eyes of the law, any other moral choices and resulting relationships will be viewed as inferior. The spirit of the law tells us that the moral foundations of liberty and care are paramount. Yet the letter of the law restricts relationships to those that uphold the moral foundations of authority and sanctity.

2. The Australian Marriage Act states that marriage is:

"The union of two people to the exclusion of all others, voluntarily entered into for life.".

Nevertheless, in 1994, the Australian laws around adultery were repealed. So, while the government tells us that marriage should ideally not involve any other parties in their sexual union, the laws suggest they don't care whether extra-couple copulation is occurring. The state stipulates that fidelity should be a feature of your marital union but then leaves loyalty to spousal self-regulation. In this way, the lack of laws in this area creates mixed messages in that it appears while authorities are pushing for purity, they both expect and tolerate adultery. In this case, lawmakers make the couple sign up to the moral foundation of fairness and loyalty but have chosen then not to use their levers of behaviour modification to uphold it.

These two examples illustrate an interesting tussle across the moral foundations that reflect the moral dilemma of monogamy. As societies move further away from the religious dogmas on which they were founded and progress further into individualism, governments have been forced to back out of the private lives of their people. The term 'Nanny State' has become a derogatory term used to describe those regimes that excessively interfere in the lives of their people and create an unnecessarily burdensome regulatory regime. A thought-provoking tension results for social administrators as they are compelled to consider what values are important enough for it to enforce and which they feel can risk being frittered away by the foibles of the common folk.

Adultery Laws

Adultery is an issue with divergent judgements across jurisdictions about the appropriate level of legislation and law enforcement. In some states and nations, extra-couple copulation is still treated as a crime. In contrast, in others, infidelity is ignored by the law.

The differing opinions regarding the treatment of adultery are no clearer observed than in the USA. Unlike the name suggests, the United States has various conflicting views regarding adultery. In recent years, several states have decided to no longer interfere in the issue of infidelity and have repealed their adultery laws. At the time of writing, these states include New Hampshire, Colorado, and West Virginia. Additionally, the states of Texas, Connecticut, Alaska, Arkansas, Iowa, Kentucky, Nebraska, Nevada, New Jersey, Oklahoma, Oregon, Vermont, and California have no-fault-based divorce systems, meaning that adultery is not considered in divorce proceedings.

In contrast, in other states, adultery is still considered illegal, with some states even prosecuting it as a criminal offence. While, for example, in New York, adultery is considered a Class B misdemeanour, in Michigan, the adulterer can be fined $5,000 and jailed for up to four years. In South Carolina, the punishment is more lenient, with a fine of only $500 and imprisonment for one year.

The good news is that where criminal penalties do exist, they are not often enforced. Instead, intimate indiscretions are used by the wronged spouse to progress a fault-based divorce. They may be used to disfavour the adulterer in a property settlement, alimony and child custody decisions. Moreover, in certain states, adultery also provides the aggrieved party the opportunity to seek retribution under civil homewrecking laws. In Hawaii, Illinois, Mississippi, New Mexico, North Carolina, South Dakota, or Utah, a person committing adultery may be liable for damages under statutes known as 'homewrecker' or 'heart balm' laws. And the damages may be extreme. In 2011, an aggrieved wife sued her husband's lover for 'alienation of affection' and was awarded $30 million in compensation. In 2010, a jury awarded a wife $9 million from her cheating husband's mistress after finding that the other woman ruined her 33-year marriage.

The upshot in the United States is that the law's role in monogamy depends very much on where you live. In some states, if you break your vow of sexual exclusivity, there may be no legal consequences (although there will always be significant psychological ones). In others, you could pay heavily for breaking the bonds of marriage as your spouse the could use the justice system to seek hefty personal and pecuniary payback.

Unlike the mixed approach in the USA, the United Kingdom and Australia have systems of no-fault divorce at a federal level. Australia was a leader in stepping out of people's private lives, implementing the no-fault divorce approach in 1975. In 1994, laws were also enacted to declare that sexual conduct between consenting adults (18 years or older) is their own personal and private matter, irrespective of marital status. There are no homewrecking laws either, so adultery then is an issue for the couple to manage as they see fit and without interference or direction from the government.

The United Kingdom was a little later to the party, only instigating a no-fault divorce system in 2022. Now, the only ground for divorce in the UK is the irretrievable breakdown of the relationship. Claims of, or the actual occurrence of infidelity, now play no role in the separation process and do not influence the division of assets and child custody.

What Constitutes Adultery?

For those jurisdictions where cheating is still a crime, how do you know when it has occurred? We covered the intricacies of infidelity in Chapter 1, but now, let's look at it through a legal lens. It is fair to say that legalising same-sex marriage has introduced a problem with how the law defines adultery. The state of New York defines adultery as sexual intercourse with someone other than the person's legal spouse. The dictionary definition of intercourse is contact. On the surface, it appears that these laws would cover contact between the genitalia of any gender combination and seemingly support same-sex unions. However, the actual definition of sexual intercourse in the New York penal code is an "act that includes any penetration of the female sex organ by the male sex organ."[53]

The restricted definition makes it impossible for same-sex couples to take advantage of any adultery clauses in separation statutes unless their partner's infidelity was conducted with a person of the opposite sex. Until the introduction of the no-fault divorce process in 2022, this definition of sexual intercourse was also found in the UK, where the law specified adultery as a husband or wife having sexual intercourse with someone of the opposite sex.

Perhaps governments are removing themselves from the bedroom in recognition of the complexity involved in determining when adultery occurs. It is relatively easy for traditional heterosexual relationships. You simply define adultery as the act of penis-in-vagina sex. Nevertheless, my mind boggles with the burden of proof for this accusation. But how do you define sexual intercourse for same-sex couples? And what do you do about all of those other acts of intimacy that could be considered cheating but do not meet the definition of adultery? What about oral sex or mutual masturbation? What about great feelings of longing, desire and love? Well, it appears many modern governments are sensible enough not to get involved in this dilemma! They leave this one well and truly alone, for there are far too many grey areas regarding physical and emotional intimacy.

Marriage Laws

While there still may be some disparity in laws enforcing sexual exclusivity (and punishing infidelity), in Western nations, there appears to be a universal commitment to prohibiting polygamy. And despite recently broadening the definition of marriage to same-sex couples, there seems very little appetite to enlarge the institution to embrace more than two people.

Having more than one legal spouse is committing the offence of bigamy. In Australia, this can carry a maximum penalty of five years imprisonment. In the United Kingdom, the prison sentence is up to a maximum of seven years. Note that this offence only occurs if an attempt to contract a legally recognised marriage exists. People can live in polyamorous relationships but cross the legal line if they attempt to formalise them under the law.

We see movement in law, though, in the decriminalisation of bigamy. For many states in America, just like in Australia and the UK, polygamy is also a crime punishable by fines, imprisonment, or both. However, in 2020, the state of Utah passed a bill reducing the penalty for polygamy from a felony to an infraction, which holds similar penalties to a speeding ticket[54]. So, while having more than one legal spouse is still illegal, it is viewed as a much lesser moral failure. This reduction in penalty was an important step forward for a community that, thanks to its Mormon pioneers, had a long history with plural marriages. Softening sanctions has allowed for greater honesty and inclusivity of lifestyles. It has also provided greater support for those suffering from domestic violence in polygamist relationships. These people, predominantly women, no longer have to fear criminal penalties on top of their personal trauma.

I am constantly in awe that despite how much our society has shifted over the recent decades, the institution of marriage is still seen as the ultimate expression of love. While so many couples choose not to worry about weddings, marriage still appears to formalise love in the eyes of the couple and society. There seems to be an assumption made that if you are not wed to your partner, then it is not a serious, committed relationship. Despite knowing that around one in every two couple will divorce, and so marriage is only a short-term arrangement, describing your relationship as de facto can still denigrate the quality of the connection in the eyes of the community in which they live.

The public power vested in the institution of marriage is evident in the petition by the Polyamory Action Lobby to the Australian Federal Parliament in 2013. It stated:

"For too long has Australia denied people the right to marry the ones they care about. We find this abhorrent. We believe

that everyone should be allowed to marry their partners, and that the law should never be a barrier to love. And that's why we demand nothing less than the full recognition of polyamorous families."[55]

For those who have chosen the path of alternative intimate relationships, the law has a very important role to play - validating and supporting their freedom and their families.

Do the laws work?

It does not look like the Polyamory Action Lobby will have success in their plight any time soon. There is an ingrained public perception that polygamy is bad for society and monogamy is the gold standard of morality. One reason is that polygamy has been traditionally associated with the abuse of women and children, and politicians are averse to being linked with arrangements tainted by exploitation and mistreatment.

This line of argument implies that monogamy is a morally superior relationship model that prevents violence against women and children. What a load of rubbish. Within monogamous relationships, we are witnessing a continual escalation in family and domestic violence, with the victims predominantly females[56]. In 2021-22, domestic violence caused almost 73,000 to seek assistance from homeless services[57], and on average, every nine days, a woman was killed by a current or former partner[58]. These statistics sadly acknowledge that exploitation and mistreatment are found in monogamous, state-sanctioned relationships as well. Sexually exclusive relationships offer no protection from the profound and traumatic effects of domestic and family violence.

Governments have also put forward the following three imperatives to justify prohibitions against adultery and bigamy:

1. The preservation of the institution of marriage.
2. The prevention of disease and illegitimate children.
3. Safeguarding of general community morals.

We can safely claim the law has failed to preserve the institution of marriage. As the following graphs show, there is a palpable trend away from marriage in the United States and an increased reliance on registered relationships in Australia.

Figure 9 - Marriage trends

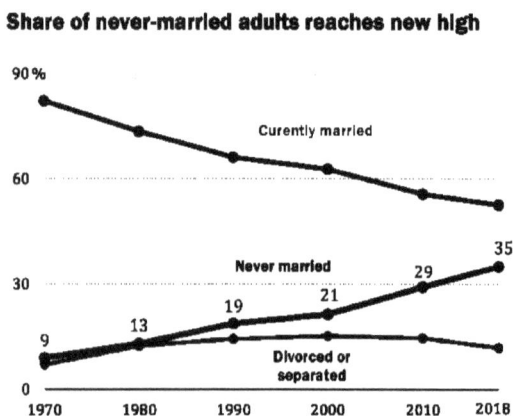

Share of never-married adults reaches new high

Notes: Based on adults ages 25-50. A small share of widowed adults is not shown.
Source: U.S. Census and American Community Survey, IPUMS .

Institute for
Family Studies

Number of registered relationships in Australia, 2016 to 2020

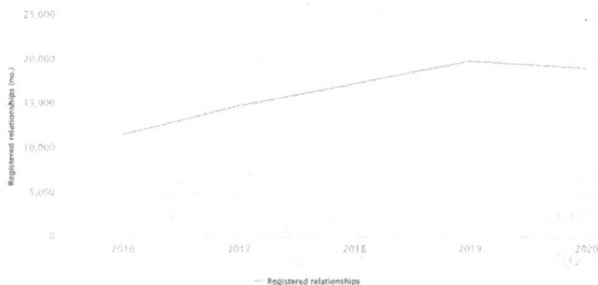

Source: Australian Bureau of Statistics, Marriages and Divorces, Australia 2020

The legalisation of divorce and the latter introduction of no-fault fractures have practically made the institution of marriage irrelevant. As discussed by Adam Phillips, it inserts a get-out clause into the marriage contract, nullifying its magnitude and minimising the consequences of failure. He states that no-fault divorce delivers:

"Optimism in assuming that better things may be coming down the line. If get-out clauses lack commitment, they also underwrite and openness about the future. My get-out clause, contracted publicly, or reassuringly affirmed in the apparent privacy of my own mind, is my uncertainty about my own desire. Only God, presumably, has no need of such things."[59]

Liberal attitudes towards divorce erode the goal of maintaining the importance of marriage. While, under the legislation, marriage is an arrangement entered into for life, we all really know that this mandate is meaningless because the option for divorce on a no-fault basis is always available. In this way, it could be said that the lawmakers themselves have decried the sanctity of this once-sacred institution.

The belief that monogamy prevented disease and illegitimate children is also an archaic notion, relevant only in those days when your first and last sexual encounters were with your spouse. Nowadays, before promises of sexual exclusivity, people of all sexual persuasions are technically free to be as promiscuous as their principles allow. With the median age of marriage now around the mid-30s, this creates a large space for sleeping around, sharing STDs and surprise pregnancies.

The statistics also show that adultery is still prevalent despite people committing to enter marriage to the exclusion of all others. Consequently, many governments have given up on their ability to enforce fidelity. Removing laws around adultery has unlikely fuelled an upsurge in cheating but merely facilitated a reduction in the profits of lawyers seeking advantage from a spouse's lust for revenge.

I would also present the prevalence of pornography as an example of how laws around adultery and bigamy have very little influence over modern-day community morals. Internet porn has much more authority over our intimate lives than our consideration of whether a decision to break vows may result in a legal penalty. It is the height of hypocrisy to condone (through inaction) the violent and oppressive modern pornography that leads to disrespectful relationships and domestic violence while telling others that they cannot formalise relationships with people they love.

The laws confuse marriage with morality. They fail to recognise that within many legal marriages, there is immorality, as spouses are abused, oppressed and subjected to coercive control and violence. They also fail to recognise that many 'illegal' relationships are founded upon deep respect, love and care. Legal marriages are not necessarily more loving than those insinuated to be immoral. Therefore, perhaps the precious time of our power brokers would be better spent on finding ways to nurture respectful relationships rather than quibble over the form they take.

Core Concepts

Laws reflect societal values but often lag behind cultural shifts.

Sometimes, laws can create rather than resolve moral conflicts in relationships.

In Australia, the Sex Discrimination Act supports diverse relationship choices, yet the Marriage Act embeds discrimination by only making marriage available for monogamous unions.

While marriage laws in Australia and similar Western nations uphold monogamy, adultery is not criminalised, creating mixed messages about the importance of sexual exclusivity in marriage.

The definition of adultery, often tied to traditional heterosexual intercourse, creates legal complications for same-sex marriages and other non-traditional relationships, leading some governments to avoid legislating personal intimacy.

Laws that aim to uphold monogamy often fail in their broader goals, as seen in the decline of marriage rates, the prevalence of divorce, and ongoing issues like family violence, which occur in monogamous unions.

The focus on maintaining monogamy through legal constraints ignores the deeper need for promoting respectful, caring relationships, regardless of their form. Instead, it reinforces a confused moral landscape where legal marriages may lack love and 'illegal' relationships may embody it.

Chapter 11 – What's Sex Got to Do with It?

Everything. Sex has everything to do with monogamy.

There is no definition of monogamy without reference to sex, as it is the practice of sexual exclusivity that is the central premise of a monogamous union. In this way, sex is embedded within and essential to the discussion of monogamy.

Sex is the motive for entering monogamous arrangements. Ironically, it is also one of the main reasons we choose to get out of them. It can be the glue that binds the couple, body and soul or the wedge that is the source of the split. When we promise to give ourselves solely to another, we are seen to be demonstrating the highest form of love and devotion, surpassed only by the formalisation of this vow through marriage.

However, the opposite is also true. Suppose the promise is broken, and one partner enjoys sexual pleasure with another. In that case, they have committed the ultimate betrayal and an immoral transgression that destroys all trust. Or, if one partner no longer wishes to share themselves sexually, then the door is opened to a world of doubt about continued attraction and enduring love. The sexual alignment between the couple, then, is critical to the ongoing flourishing of their exclusive bond.

It Is Never Just Sex

If sex were simply a physical act of procreation or pleasure, our lives would be simple. However, sex is never just sex. It is a notion and an act laden with enormous baggage, handed down from our ancestors and potentially added to by the adults who saw us through our formative years.

Whether we are willing to admit it or not, sex is inherently intermingled with our individual identities. Attracting a sexual partner, keeping them loyal and satisfying them are all feats that society says make us successful, and so become inextricably interwoven into our evaluations of self-importance. Therefore, while we may like to think that sex is merely a physical act of pleasure or procreation, the human consciousness is far too complex.

Sex is a showcase for our loftiest aspirations and our deepest anxieties.

When Sex Subverts

The immature psychological and emotional inputs from each partner can mean that sex becomes less about the celebration and connection of the couple and more about respite from or treatment of our traumas and insecurities. I have seen three main ways in which sex in monogamous unions has been used to address anxieties, being when:
1. Sex is used as a confirmation of self-worth.
2. Monogamy is used covertly for sexual certainty.
3. Sex is used as a weapon with which to wield power.

Securing Self-Worth

As suggested previously, the act of sex can be drenched in insecurity. In fact, I have heard it said that it is through sex that you get to truly witness your partner's neuroses. Because, during sex, we expose ourselves and become vulnerable physically but also emotionally. We put our bodies in danger of injury, judgment and criticism. And even more profoundly, we risk rejection and the monstrous melancholy that comes with the thought that we are not worthy of being loved.

If, as Dr Keegan suggests, most adults are still stuck in the socialised mind, then it is likely that for most people, denial of sex will cut to the core of self-confidence. We begin to question our beauty, strength, and carnal desirability. In an instant, we are submerged into our deepest, darkest fear – of being unlovable and doomed to be alone. Our partner's sexual response becomes either a confirmation or denial of our value to them, the tribe, and society in general. With a lack of self-awareness and maturity, our partner's behaviour can instigate paranoia, suspicion, depression, withdrawal and mistrust.

If sex wanes in a relationship, those in the socialised mind will likely take this pattern personally. The result may well be withdrawal, self-protection and separation. Through conjoining sex and self-worth, confusion can reign and create a murky swamp of sensual dissatisfaction and emotional distress. This response, though, is both selfish and egocentric. It refuses to consider the wellbeing of the partner and the reasons why they may not feel like participating in this act of connection. Our lives are incredibly complex and full of external and internal pressures, impacting the energy we bring into our relationships. By avoiding considering our partner's problems and leaping straight into the mire of self-pity, we are unfortunately only demonstrating our inability to care for the wellbeing of the one we profess to love.

Likewise, suppose it is us experiencing reduced sex drive. In that case, it can be difficult to understand or admit to the reasons for this situation. All the images we see in the media portray a lack of sex drive as a weakness, as the walkway into spinsterhood or the hallway to a hermitage. Unfortunately, surrounded by this myriad of messages, it is easy to see frigidity as a failure. It can seem much easier to permit our partner to seek sex elsewhere than to dig deep and investigate our fallibility. I wonder how many 'open marriages' are created because the couple was unwilling to have courageous conversations about their impediments to sexual vibrancy.

The dilemma that arises from equating sex with self-worth is that when our sex lives change (as the laws of nature tell us they will), we can let fear creep in, use it to withdraw from the relationship and replace passion with self-protection. If this occurs, then the opportunity is missed to lean in and explore each other at a much deeper level. By allowing fear to pull us back, we do not get to peer into our deepest desires nor investigate structures and systems that keep us stuck. Wallowing in self-pity and floundering in failure becomes a convenient distraction to exploring our innermost worlds and finding those sources of worth that do not depend on the adoration of others.

Seeking Sexual Certainty

I am unsure whether anyone would admit to this, but entering a monogamous relationship could be seen as a very self-serving mechanism for assured sex. Having someone beside you in bed is much easier than spending days and nights patronising pubs, dallying at discos or meandering in meetup groups. Securing a sexual partner is certainly a motivation for monogamy, and while technically legitimate is both disrespectful and demeaning.

With this view, sex becomes an unwritten term in the relationship contract and dictates that one or both partners have the right to sex. After all, isn't that why they got married? Not providing sex becomes a breach of contract and, for some, a legitimate reason to terminate the agreement. With this belief, sex is quickly turned from an openhearted offering of the self to a form of oppression and obligation. I know of women and men who describe marriage as a form of bonded prostitution. While this may seem harsh, it speaks to how sex can become an expectation rather than an expression of love.

Sex As A Source Of Supremacy

The similarity of the words monogamy and monopoly is worth considering, as is the comparison of their consequences. Years of economic experience tell us that when there is only one player in any market, there is always domination, duress, control, and coercion. In these situations, governments may declare 'market failure' and intervene to protect the less-powerful parties.

Employing this analogy, we can view monogamy as a situation where there is only one person in your market providing sex. As the person wanting sex, this places you in a position of great vulnerability and at the whim of the sex provider. However, in the world of the couple, no governments are willing to intercede to prevent market failure. It is up to the individual to deal with the power imbalance. They can do this by giving up power and either living in submission or exiting the sex market altogether. Or they can attempt to redress the power imbalance by:

- Asserting domination or control over the source of sexual pleasure, either physically or psychologically.
- Finding alternate providers of sex to lessen the partner's monopoly and power.

Monogamous relationships are often entered into to create a source of support and nurturing for each individual. However, through the monopoly over sex, they become a pure portrayal of Hegel's dialectic – two consciousnesses meet, and they begin a struggle for dominance. If one consciousness overpowers the other, they enter into a master-slave relationship[60].

Navigating Nature

No matter how evolved we may consider ourselves to be, we cannot escape our biology or the laws of nature. Concerning monogamous relationships, it is inevitable that we will see shifts in levels of sexual energy over time and that we may experience new sources of sexual stimulation. These situations in themselves are not problematic. Issues arise through the decisions we make on how we deal with them.

When Sex Wanes

Some rampant romantics may want to change this title to 'if sex wanes' to suggest it is not a preordained predicament. But let's get real and view sexual desire like any other energy on this planet. As the Hermetic Law of Rhythm tells us, it ebbs and flows. Like the tides, the seasons, and circadian rhythms – there is a flow and an oscillation to our lives. It is natural for there to be waves of sexual vibrancy and a push towards connection, and there will be lulls of withdrawal where celibacy and solace are needed. The outward movement of adventure and expedition will naturally seek to be balanced with the desire for retreat, contemplation and restoration of energy. And the deep desire to be embraced within a partnership will fluctuate with the fight to regain our individuality and independence.

It is not just the laws of nature that we have to deal with, but our biology. The hormones that have us lusting after our partner dwindle over time, making it harder to sustain sexual desire. There is no doubt also that the cortisol level generated by our busy lives would contribute to feelings of fatigue and fear, making sex feel like just another task to tick off the to-do list.

However, we are surrounded by media that warns any waning of sexual desire is cause for alarm bells. In our modern lives, where the measure of success is progress, not 'getting' sex is akin to failure. Moreover, if we equate the sexual responsiveness of our partner with our self-worth or sense of power, then any rejection of sexual advances will automatically cause us to feel threatened, afraid, and unfulfilled.

If we expect sex as part of the marriage contract, then its lack of provision by our partner would also be viewed as a betrayal. For so many, sex is a symbol not only of attraction but of validation and acceptance. Being seen as a worthy mate is so entrenched in our psyche that rejection of sexual advances becomes automatically associated with the rejection of the entire person and an indication of their lack of value.

These insecurities have some people leaping to unhelpful responses to sexual decline. There may be the belief that a lack of sex also means there is a lack of love, leading people to conclude that the relationship is over. One or both partners may withdraw and begin the process of self-protection, maybe even readying the psychological and emotional lifeboats.

I feel I must address two common ways a couple tries to reinvigorate their sex lives and the dangers that lie within. The first is to expand their sexual circle by inviting another sexual player or joining with other partners in Swinger's events. Undoubtedly, the novelty and excitement of these adventures give the couple something to talk about and may get their heart racing. However, suppose either one or both are bringing insecurity and anxiety into their sexual lives and entering this activity out of fear. In that case, it will likely result in only further challenges to their psychological and emotional wellbeing. Increasing the number of people in a sexual relationship is a sure way to spice things up. Still, each extra person also brings more complexity to the connections. It may create a short-term alliance between the 'us' of the couple and the 'them' of the new entrant. Still, the triad will only succeed if the original alliance is strong. Otherwise, it could breed further mistrust and suspicion and lead to outright civil war.

Some couples also turn to pornography to stimulate their sexual appetites, hoping that watching others play out sexual fantasies may inspire them to do the same. There is certainly nothing wrong with engaging the imagination of others to help bring more vigour into a relationship. The danger here, though, is that porn may damage the connection the couple so desperately wished to darn. Porn itself is completely unrealistic. From the five-hour hard-ons to the woman enjoying ejaculation on her face, porn is fundamentally a presentation of power. If one of the partners feels powerless, they may also feel compelled to act out some role-plays, leading to further feelings of shame, guilt and suppression.

Suppose one cannot live up to the unrealistic prowess presented in porn. In that case, it may further reduce sexual confidence and increase self-loathing. These responses push the couple further apart rather than uniting them in exciting exploration. Perhaps instead of turning to more unnatural and external methods of enhancing their sex lives, the couple could turn to each other and examine how their lives may be suppressing the natural vivacity of their spirits.

When Desire Wanders

Another key aspect regarding sex in monogamous relationships is the angst that arises when one partner desires someone else. We may be operating under the ludicrous assumption that monogamy is natural. Therefore, we see the lust for another as evidence of our weak or faulty nature. We may wonder what is wrong with us when, despite having a loving relationship and admiring our partner greatly, we still have sexual feelings for a friend, a colleague or a staff member at the local café. We may even use these events to criticise ourselves and fuel the belief that we are not worthy of the great love bestowed upon us. If our partner knows we desire another, then they may quickly be sucked into the whirlpool of self-doubt, wondering whether their partner still finds them attractive.

What if I told you, though, those sexual feelings do not necessarily mean that you want to have hot sex with the person that arouses them? Sure, they may pull you towards manifesting this. However, the feelings are more than just physical urges. They hold incredible messages about what is missing in our lives. By dismissing, repressing, or acting out on them without first investigating them fully, we are losing a valuable opportunity to know ourselves more deeply and to bring more compassion rather than conflict into our lives.

Sexual feelings are just one of five major emotions studied by Jim Dethmer[61]. His work has focused on helping people identify emotions as they arise and distil the wisdom they bring. It is common for people to be afraid of sexual feelings, worrying that they are calling us to break our vows or that they indicate we are some sexual deviant. However, Jim Dethmer would suggest that the desire for sex is, at its very core, a calling to create.

When we feel horny, the initial thought is that we want sex. However, the message that Jim Dethmer wants us to get is that it is not always copulation that forces the feelings but a more profound pull to create something, to bring forth an intimate and inimitable expression of our existence. For at its heart, sex represents the ultimate creative force. Through sex, two individuals are merged, and their union initiates an entirely new energy. Through procreation, sex creates the miracle of a new and unique life. In this way, sex embodies vitality, is at the centre of creation and is the inspiration for artists of every generation.

So instead of dismissing desire for another as evidence of your own or your partner's sexual deviancy, perhaps it should first be used as a prompt to question what new ideas, innovations and creativity are required in your life. Have you lost connection with your own sense of passion and purpose for life? Is the person you desire just representing what you are lacking in yourself? Suppose the couple is committed to maintaining the vows of monogamy. In that case, these questions can be shared to develop collaborative and constructive responses to sexual urges that arise from outside.

They can use these feelings to craft a life that seeks to sustain the appreciation for beauty, the vitality of desire and the strength of their sexuality.

Core Concepts

Monogamy revolves around the concept of sexual exclusivity, making sex a central aspect of the relationship.

Sex is both a motivation for entering and a reason for exiting monogamous unions. It can strengthen the bond or drive a wedge between partners.

Sex carries significant emotional and psychological weight beyond physical pleasure or procreation. It is closely tied to personal identity, self-worth, and societal perceptions of success.

Sex is often misused within monogamous relationships, serving as a tool to address insecurities or exert control rather than as a means of connection.

Sexual desire naturally fluctuates due to biological and emotional factors. A decline in sexual energy is normal but can create fear and misinterpretation.

Common strategies to rekindle sexual desire, such as introducing third parties or using pornography, often fail to address underlying insecurities and can exacerbate feelings of inadequacy or mistrust.

Attraction to others outside the relationship is natural and not necessarily indicative of a lack of love or commitment. Such feelings should be explored for deeper understanding rather than dismissed or acted upon impulsively. They often signal desires for creativity and pursuit of individual passions.

Chapter 12 – Monogamy by Choice?

When it comes to intimate relationships, there are many different arrangements possible. There are four dimensions that can be manipulated along continuums to create a significant number of alternative models. These relationship dimensions are:

1. Number of people.
2. Extent of sexual intimacy.
3. Degree of emotional commitment.
4. Degree of formalisation.

At one extreme, a person may remain single and celibate, deciding that the only sexual connection they will create will be with themselves. Or in contrast, several people could have a loving, committed, and sexual relationship and have formalised their obligations to each other in some form of a legally binding contract. As we have seen in the previous chapter, this cannot be through marriage.

The range of routes (pardon the pun) is shown in the following diagram.

Figure 10 - Intimate relationship variables

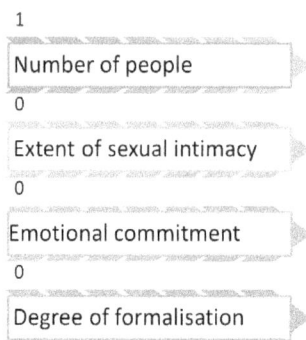

1

Number of people

0

Extent of sexual intimacy

0

Emotional commitment

0

Degree of formalisation

As is clear from this diagram, monogamy is only one very simple setting on this connection control panel. So why does it continue to be seen as the most credible choice of relationship arrangements? Certainly, the influence of Christianity has been considerable and has embedded monogamy as a major moral standard.

In addition, the laws of Western nations still ban bigamy, sending a clear signal that alternative arrangements are amoral. However, approximately half of the population now does not align with any religion. And suppose you are not worried about formalising your relationships. In that case, nothing in the law stops you from progressing with polygamy. Then why, despite it being against our natural tendencies, do most people continue down the coupledom corridor? What is it about this paradigm that continues to make it so pervasive?

Causes Of Coupledom

I believe four key causes compel people to choose coupledom. These are:

1. To alleviate pressure
2. To attain pleasure
3. Pragmatism
4. Prejudice.

Alleviating Pressure

We all like to think of ourselves as independent thinkers controlling our futures. The reality is that most of us operate from a Socialised Mind, meaning that we are more concerned with other people's opinions of us than we are about pursuing our own unique goals and potential. The result is that even if we are not aware of it, our choices in each area of our lives are influenced by what we think others may think, say, or do and by the fear of being rejected by them.

We have seen that monogamy is the 'normal' relationship model and is viewed as the gold standard of morality. And as much as we may profess that we don't care what other people think, deep down, our tribal brains and hearts know that being normal means survival - physically and psychologically. Isolation and loneliness are the antitheses of wellbeing, so why would we risk putting ourselves in this situation and being ostracised from the tribe?

This subconscious pressure can compel people to follow the crowd and forgo questioning their values and aspirations. It is an unseen force that conceals any other choice but those endorsed by friends, family, and those they follow on social media. By subscribing to the same relationship arrangements as a society, the tension that comes with non-conformity is eradicated, making our lives more comfortable.

Attaining Pleasure

It's often said that authentic relationships are the epitome of joy and the pinnacle of human achievement. Despite the ongoing debate about the relevance of monogamy, the joy of loving and being loved is undeniable. To be truly seen, admired, adored, understood, and deeply appreciated by another is a glorious experience. And to reciprocate these feelings is equally satisfying. The feeling of safety, care, and trust in another person is both luminous and liberating.

There is contentment to be found in the sense of security that monogamy brings and a strength that comes with marriage's legal bonds. Of course, while I would argue that the sense of security and surety are delusional (you can never truly know another person, and divorce is always possible), they ease the anxiety that comes with the uncertainty of being a free agent. There is also an incredible confidence to be gained from being one of the tribe, and an opportunity then to be a source of wisdom and guidance for the children and grandchildren that will need comforting through the challenges of coupledom.

Pragmatism

So many aspects of our modern materialistic lives make monogamy the most practical relationship model. Our busy lives mean there is very little time to find just one person who is true partnership material, let alone two or three! And very few people have the cash to splash on courting several suitors. Pooling and coordinating resources are also much easier with just one other person. While adding others to the economic relationship may create greater potential for financial security and wealth, it also increases the expenditure and complexity of cash management. Scheduling the work commitments and social lives of two people can be difficult. Where children are involved, their care and extra-curricular activities can result in calendar chaos. Adding more people onto the agenda only compounds the challenges and may make maintaining sanity impossible.

Managing schedules is a walk in the park compared to the effort required to traverse other people's psychological and emotional lives. Given the intensity involved in dealing with the other's sun and shadows, it is understandable that people would select to keep their lives simple and enter the emotional roller coaster with just one other rider.

The relative stability of a monogamous relationship is also seen to be optimal for child-rearing. Parental responsibilities and inheritances are clear and simple, which certainly works well in theory. However, the number of children suffering through divorce and in 'broken' families suggests the reality is not so clear cut. The evidence illustrates that it is not monogamy that directly influences a positive identity and independence in the child but the love and acceptance provided to them by their caregivers. Monogamy does not make for happy children. Happy, healthy parents make for happy, healthy children and these can be found in all types of relationship arrangements.

Prejudice

The entire socio-economic system in Western nations is established to support monogamous relationships. Having more than one marriage under the law is illegal. However, people can still establish their own less formal relationship arrangements. The reality is that this may not even be a consideration due to the lack of endorsement and provision for alternative arrangements.

Every piece of paperwork you complete only has spaces for one other person, be it spouse, partner, de facto, emergency contact or next of kin. This situation may be a minor inconvenience to those wishing to live in non-monogamous and committed relationships. However, it is also an insidious reminder that they don't fit the mould of what society considers right or just.

And as long as there are bigamy laws in place, then there is the inference that those who desire anything other than monogamy are faulty, improper, and immoral. This judgement is exacerbated in those countries and states where there are criminal penalties in place. The mere presence of these laws implies those who do not follow the monogamy bandwagon as wicked, aberrant and requiring correction. It is understood that the laws must uphold the moral standard of the state. But how can a law truly impose conditions on loving relationships? And how can a law itself be considered moral if it restricts the free expression and formalisation of an adult, consensual and caring relationship?

The lack of social structures and systemic support for alternatives beyond monogamy can be a significant barrier for people to pursue any other possibility. Perhaps it may be intentional on the part of politicians and their policy advisors. Nevertheless, it is cruel conduct towards a component of their constituency and a constraint on mature consensual commitments.

Are We Free To Choose?

Technically, we can choose any relationship arrangement that takes our fancy - even multiple concurrent marriages. We just have to bear the consequences. If we choose polygamy, then we must also be willing, unfortunately, to wear the penalties associated with the crime of bigamy. If we choose monogamy out of fear, we must bear the consequences of internal and relationship conflict.

However, this generalisation is a simplistic notion that does not consider the level of maturity and social situation of each individual making the decision. As we have seen in the Dr Keegan Model of Adult Development, a significant proportion of the population is beholden to social pressure, so they may feel they have no other choice. Likewise, there are some that, due to financial or cultural constraints, also have their ability to choose curtailed.

Some people have no legitimate capacity or capability to acknowledge any alternatives, let alone act on them. There are some for who monogamy is a 'must' rather than a 'should' or 'could'. There are those then who are oppressed either by their peers or their own paranoia. In this case, the moral foundations of care and liberty have to be sacrificed for the allegiance and authority that will secure their safety. There are those for which loyalty, lethargy or lack of introspection conceals any other choice but to continue into coupledom. In this situation, monogamy is done 'to' a person rather than the format chosen 'for' their growth and flourishing.

In contrast, there are those with the wisdom and will to relegate social convention to second place and for whom their truth comes up trumps. When faced with entering a monogamous relationship, these people have three possible pathways.

1. Through reflection and deep consideration, they understand that monogamy is important to them and aligns with who they truly are. They enter a monogamous relationship believing in the value of this arrangement and agreeing with their partner that sexual exclusivity is the model through which they will grow, thrive, and reach their full potential as individuals and as a pair. They work stoically with their partner to maintain their vow

and do so until the dissolution of the relationship, either through death or divorce.

2.   Through the same process of reflection and contemplation, they realise that they are confused about the notion of monogamy and have doubts about their ability to keep the pledge of sexual exclusivity. They discuss these concerns with their partner before embarking on the bonds of monogamy. Then, suppose they decide to continue with the relationship. In that case, it is done freely and fully, with the acknowledgement that each person will grow and change and that this model may not always be conducive to their individual evolution.

3.   As per the previous scenario, the person doubts the importance of and/or their ability to keep the pledge of sexual exclusivity. However, they choose not to discuss these concerns with their partner because they are either scared or selfish (or both). They vow with words, but their hearts are not fully in it. Through silence, these people have born false witness to their partners and failed to disclose an internal conflict that affects their 'loved one' now and in the future. If they decide to have sexual relationships outside the partnership, then any lies used to cover up cheating have further consolidated a relationship founded upon falsehoods.

In all three situations, a person has employed their free will and exercised choice concerning coupledom. However, only in the first two scenarios were the choices made with honesty, care and complete information. In the latter, the decision was made to withhold some crucial conditions on which the relationship was created. The person has not shown their true selves to their partner and given them a chance to love them despite their doubts and support them through their scepticism. In choosing not to reveal their reality, they have taken away the ability of the other to make a completely considered choice as to whether this relationship is right for them at this time. It presents a sense of surety and safety that is deceptive. In this way, the lack of openness and honesty is an act of treason, and monogamy is founded on immorality.

Only when a person knows their truth and speaks their truth can intimacy be founded upon integrity and careful choices be made. Without this, choices are not fully informed. The relationship is represented by falsities and facades that will only rot the foundations of faithfulness.

Only the first two scenarios provide a path to loving relationships and eudemonic happiness. Neither guarantees the relationship will deliver a happily ever after. Still, in living true to one's values, there is much more respect and care for self and others. There is more honesty and authenticity and less potential for alarming surprises, sinister shocks and bitterness if the world we contrived falls apart.

Making Conscious Choices

The three scenarios outlined above contain one central tenet – that people consciously make choices regarding coupledom. They rely on people being intimate with their ideals, dreams and doubts and aware of when these are being challenged. It necessitates someone being alert to the stimulus and cognisant of the space for choice. It depends on the person's ability to identify the integral instant they have to make decisions based on the best interests of all involved. The outcome depends on the person's proficiency in pinpointing their moment of power and whether they wish to use it to produce pain or peace. This level of mindfulness is an admirable aspiration.

In contrast, our approach to relationships is often like undertaking a spontaneous sailing adventure. We enter relationships so willingly but without discussions and considerations about what we are committing to and how these commitments fit with our true selves. We jump aboard, buoyed by the thrill of a new adventure, but without first checking whether anyone knows how to sail. In our excitement to be embraced by another, we forget to check the sturdiness of the ship. The bliss of romance may also blind us to the gaping holes in the hull and the disrepair of the navigation device.

We are so desperate to love and be loved that we fail to consider the landing and logistics that this loving may require. We don't generally take time to discuss and agree on the destination we are working towards, the values we share (and those we don't), and how receptive each of us is to changing course and/or the structure of the ship itself. We sail off into the sunset without clear plans about how we may weather the storms or manage mutiny.

Sure, through prenuptial agreements, we can ensure sufficient lifeboats in case of emergency. We may also have a friendly flotation device waiting in the wings if we need to abandon the ship. But without conscious co-creation, the adventure becomes an exercise in ad-hoc adaptation. In my mind, this is a wicked waste of the precious resources each person brings to the pair. Time is our greatest asset, and throwing this away without a thought is a tragedy. Conscious collaboration, purposeful planning and skilled seamanship are the only things that will create the potential for this adventure to be safe, satisfying and self-sustaining.

Core Concepts

Monogamy is one of many relationship arrangements available, with options varying by the number of people involved, the level of sexual intimacy, the degree of emotional commitment, and the extent of formalisation.

The four main reasons people choose monogamy are: to alleviate social pressure, to attain pleasure, pragmatism, and prejudice. Monogamy is often seen as the easiest relationship option due to societal expectations, emotional fulfillment, logistical simplicity, and systemic support.

While individuals technically have the freedom to choose their relationship arrangements, decisions are practically constrained by societal, legal, and cultural pressures.

Social pressures and the desire to conform play a significant role in people's choice of monogamy. Fear of isolation and rejection can push individuals to follow the traditional path without fully exploring their personal values and preferences.

Three pathways exist for those entering monogamous relationships: fully embracing monogamy with conviction, entering with doubts and communicating these openly, or entering with doubts about the ability to maintain monogamy but not disclosing these concerns. Only the first two scenarios allow for authentic and respectful relationships.

Chapter 13 – A Next-Gen Model of Monogamy

Through the previous chapters, we have explored the notion of monogamy from many different perspectives. I have traversed monogamy in the physical, mental, and spiritual realms. I have seen the pressures placed upon it from the partnerships of the past, the practicalities of the present and have gained a glimpse of future possibilities. I never could have imagined how complex the world of monogamy could be.

However, now that the journey has concluded, it is time to take a step back and see the estate in its entirety. It is time to integrate my memories of role models' past with the wisdom of all those I have encountered in writing this book. It is time to condense the complexity into a construct that can stimulate critical conversations about coupledom.

Monogamy is a relationship arrangement centred around one fundamental promise — to remain sexually exclusive to one person. The reported rates of cheating would suggest systematic issues with how this arrangement is being implemented. The regularity of divorce would also indicate that it is not a sustainable model for a lifetime. I believe that this is because the way we currently do monogamy ignores the complexity of our human desires and neglects to care for the natural laws in which the relationship operates. In pursuing what is righteous, we have tried to ignore reality. In our concentration on social conformance, we have lost consciousness, compassion and consideration.

The consequence is that for many of us, our notions of monogamy are founded upon faulty and dangerous assumptions, including that:

- Monogamy is natural for humans. It is not. Monogamy is counter to our physical and neurological processes.
- Monogamy is about completing each individual through union with another. It is not. We do not need anyone to complete us. We are already whole and worthy.
- Monogamy delivers societal stability. The number of broken families and children in counselling from traumatic break-ups would suggest otherwise.
- Monogamy is moral. How can it be moral if it oppresses the freedom of the individuals within it and restricts the flourishing of each?
- Monogamy is a demonstration of love. It can be, but it can also be used as a tool of possession, suppression and dependence.

The flawed framework has further ramifications, in that people feel they only have two choices: to suppress the fullness of their humanity and die in dull relationships or express themselves outside the bonds of their restrictive relationships. In both situations, there is suffering through suppression of the spirit or a violation of vows.

Monogamy Mk2

One thing that has become abundantly clear throughout this book is that monogamy is not a 'thing' but a notion that can be navigated wherever and however the couple sees fit. Therefore, a couple can consciously create a relationship in which neither person is torn between the black and the white but can dance together within the grey.

What could this new model of monogamy look like? Here is a simplistic and theoretical representation of my Monogamy Mk2.

Figure 11 - Monogamy Mk2

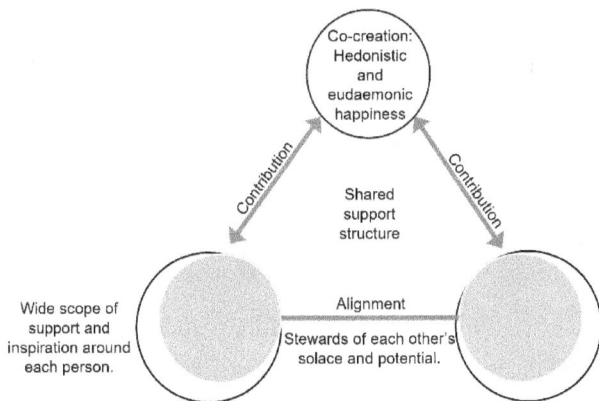

Co-creation:
Hedonistic
and
eudaemonic
happiness

Contribution

Contribution

Shared
support
structure

Wide scope of
support and
inspiration around
each person.

Alignment

Stewards of each other's
solace and potential.

I must declare, though, that this model is not my unique construct. It stands on the shoulders of giants — those who have dug deep to examine their own experiences, apply their intellect and become intimate with their own vulnerabilities. These wise friends, philosophers, psychologists and relationship experts have provided the parts. I have merely muddled them together in a way that makes sense to me. Let's work through the key features of this model of monogamy.

The Base

"Stand together, yet not too near together: for the pillars of the temple stand apart" — Kahlil Gibran.

This model's base was initially stimulated by understanding how attraction can only occur when there is a distance between two entities. Therefore, there needs to be a foundation of alignment and interaction between the individuals, but also a space that allows for the energies of each to flow and intertwine, to acknowledge and attract the other. Simone de Beauvoir was a great contributor to the base, advocating for the need to balance the commitments of coupledom with sufficient solitude to allow a person to reflect on their experiences, understand themselves and their full potential[62].

One of the greatest dangers to monogamy is the waning of sexual desire, which directly results from the lack of passion and life within the individuals themselves. If a relationship can support the expansion, growth and flourishing of each person, then in theory, it is more likely that this will flow into their sex lives and provide protection from declining desires.

"Strong emotions such as passion and bliss are indications that you're connected to Spirit, or 'inspired,' if you will.

When you're inspired, you activate dormant forces, and the abundance you seek in any form comes streaming into your life." ~ Wayne Dyer

Familiarity breeds contempt, but what if the person you are committed to is a continually changing, growing, evolving person, full of surprises and sensational achievements? In this case coupledom becomes an endless exploration, bringing a new discovery each day.

"A good marriage is that in which each appoints the other guardian of his solitude" — Rainer Maria Rilke.'

In this model, each person must be able to operate as free agents, supported to reach their full potential. However, with the commitment made to their partner, each person also becomes a steward of their spouse's solace and their partner's possibilities. Each person is there to back not only the 'being' of the other but also their 'becoming'.

Pursuing individual potential may seem selfish and suggest that each entity uses the other for its benefit. However, as the Dalai Lama may say, it is a case of 'wise selfishness', for it is clear that the strength and positivity of any relationship rely upon the integrity and inspiration of each individual. By sustaining each spouse, the coupledom has a greater chance of maintaining the vitality required to create combined value. In addition, the law of cause and effect tells us that investing in the individuals will positively affect the pair. Creating happiness in each contributes to the health of their connections. Thomas Moore believes that both coming together and standing apart are essential to a full and sustainable relationship.

"An alternative might be generously to help and accompany our lovers as daily they find some life for their deep cravings, and at the same time, equally generously to stand apart as an individual unwilling to be somebody else. This pattern reflects the openhearted surrender and aggressive distancing proper to human love." [63]

This description is a delightful depiction of how two people can recognise, respect and flow between the opposing needs that create the complexity of coupledom. It shows the swing between cherishing the comfort of closeness and respecting the role that separateness plays in sustaining the spirit.

The space around each spouse is also an important characteristic of this model. In Monogamy Mk2, each entity has its ambit of acquaintances. Esther Perel made this crucial contribution by observing that no one person can or should be expected to fulfil all of our needs. Therefore, it is imperative that our relationships operate within a community of support rather than an isolated union [64].

The alignment between the two entities in the model is essential, yet its importance can be overlooked. This alignment takes many forms, including values, focus on the moral foundations, and visions for the future. Most essentially, though, this alignment takes the form of equality. While some philosophers may argue that there has been, and always will be, a power differential in all relationships and that it is only exacerbated in the monogamous arrangement, Hegel, the instigator of the dialectic concept, thought otherwise. Hegel was wise enough to chart a way out of this dilemma, suggesting it is through the creation of:

"A mature loving unity consisting of a synthesis in which each separate lover is one organism in a living whole."[65]

With this comment, Hegel suggests that within monogamy, there can be a mixture, not a merging. An amalgamation, not an appropriation. A co-creation, not a consumption. Each person can retain their independence and, more importantly, use their agency to create something bigger, better, more influential and divine than they could alone.

The Pinnacle

James Hillman[66] added great weight to the notion of monogamy as a triangle, observing that there is always a third 'other' in any relationship. It could be a child, a career, God, a parent, an unresolved trauma or an affair. Regardless of type, there is always a third. Unfortunately, this love triangle is never always recognised and the third player remains an invisible and yet significant source of struggle. Hillman's observation got me thinking — why can't we turn this undercover entity into a conscious creation? Is there a possibility of transforming a sneaky sidekick into a shared aspiration?

"The chain of marriage is so heavy that it takes two to bear it; sometimes three." ~ Alexander Dumas

In this model, the important role of hedonistic and eudaemonic happiness is also recognised, with the latter adding depth and dignity to the relationship. The pinnacle then becomes less about profiteering from a partnership and more about supporting each person's potential.

What I love about this model is the flexibility with which the pinnacle can be defined. Ultimately, the top point of the relationship is a co-creation, a vision of what the bond between the two can build. This creation can be anything — a safe, comfortable home, financial flourishing, spiritual sex, or a family overflowing with hedonistic and eudemonic happiness. This vision can be understood to have its own flow and follow the natural laws to shift and change over time to evolve with the entities.

Conversations about what this apex looks like could be some of the most meaningful a couple could ever have, for it seeks to answer two very important questions:
1. What is it that they want to create together?
2. How can each contribute to this vision?

The other justification for the triangle shape comes from science. While people are happy to debate what takes the title as the strongest shape, there is no doubt that triangles are sturdy. This strength comes from the space between the two base corners. Its power comes from both the separateness and connection of the base entities. It is a shape that uses both compression and tension to succeed. It is magical in its ability to celebrate opposites.

Two Triangles

I am conscious that Monogamy Mk2 could be accused of being mainly masculine in nature, with the pair shown to be logically progressing upwards towards a positive outcome. Whereas it is the masculine and feminine dance that ignites life and sustains vitality. While the masculine focuses on solving problems and success, the feminine energy plays a pivotal role in creating compassion, comfort, nurturing and restoring relationships. In mythology, an inverted triangle represents this feminine flow, which is why I now propose that Monogamy Mk2 be expanded as shown on the following page.

Figure 12 - The Revised Monogamy Mk2

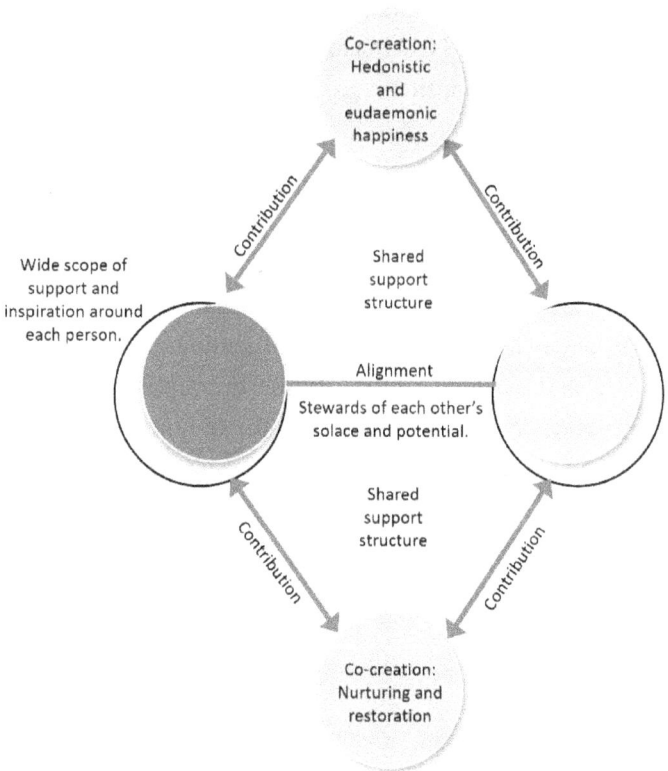

The need for dual directions is recognised in many ancient cultures. For example, in Hinduism, the Shatkona is a powerful holy symbol. The upward triangle represents the masculine deity Shiva, and the downward triangle signifies the feminine goddess Shakti. Together, they demonstrate the divine union of masculine and feminine and the source of all creation.

Figure 13 - The Shatkona

This balance is imperative to display and demonstrate in monogamous arrangements so that each individual and their creation can be supported and sustained. Just as important as achieving hedonistic happiness and progressing towards potential is concentrating on the love, compassion, and care that each person so desperately needs to survive and thrive. In this way, feminine energy is a recognised and respected input to the flourishing of the relationship.

Dependencies For Delivery Of Mk2

Monogamy Mk2 sounds fantastic in theory. It embraces the best of both worlds: independence and integration, physical wellbeing and spiritual self-actualisation, masculine drive and feminine nurturing, sturdiness, and space for sway and shift. It offers an arrangement much more aligned with the modern drive for individual independence while still recognising that we grow through our partners and communities.

For this model to be productive in practice, however, there are two pre-requisites:

1. Consciousness
2. Courage.

Consciousness

As I mentioned previously, it was through ignorance that I adopted and applied harmful beliefs about what monogamy was and could be. I was unaware of the invisible influences feeding my frameworks and forcing my feelings. This lack of awareness kept me repeating regimented and repressive relationships. So many burdens are born from not bringing our beliefs into conscious awareness, testing them, and sharing them with our significant others. We become powerless reactionaries, unaware of the pivotal moment of choice and the wide range of alternative responses.

Monogamy Mk2 can only operate with each entity aware of its values and visions for the future. It depends upon both being cognisant of the pressures they face and how they will choose to confront them. Its success relies on each person recognising, respecting, and reconciling with the model's opposites. It requires that each individual make a conscious commitment to caring for others' individuality and pursuing their potential.

In this way, Monogamy Mk2 is not just a model but an invitation to exhume expectations, bring them out into the light, and let them linger in loving kindness.

"Awareness is the greatest agent of change."
~ Eckhardt Tolle

Courage

It is said that with awareness comes responsibility. Understanding how your thoughts around monogamy taint your experience is incredibly enlightening, although relatively easy. Taking action to counter these deep-seated and destructive drivers requires courage. It needs each person to be able to feel their fears but decide that their growth and the thriving of their relationship is more important than their insecurities. Monogamy Mk2 calls on the couple to become confident with the change process and contribute all they can to co-creation. It needs each to be vulnerable and value this in the other. For the alignment to hold, it requires each to have a strong underlying imperative of understanding.

This model also requires risk-taking. Allowing your partner independence surely sparks sensations of fright, fears of abandonment, and anxiety about adultery. Disclosing hopes for your flourishing and co-creation creates the risk these will not be shared by your spouse, leaving you lingering in loneliness. Focusing on the feminine may manifest fears around feeling foolish, soft and weak. For this reason, Monogamy Mk2 will not work without courage — to try a new approach, invest in the experiment, and allow yourself to transform with each new experience.

In this way, Monogamy Mk2 is not just a chart of coupledom but a calling to live consciously, compassionately, and confidently in your spirit and nurture your partner to do the same.

"It takes courage to grow up and become who you really are." — E.E. Cummings

Core Concepts

Monogamy involves intricate dynamics and has evolved over time through influences from history, culture, and individual experiences.

Traditional monogamy is often based on flawed beliefs, such as the idea that it is natural for humans, that it completes individuals, that it guarantees societal stability, that it is inherently moral, and that it is the ultimate expression of love.

Monogamy Mk2: This updated model of monogamy allows for a flexible and conscious approach to relationships, where partners navigate between individual freedom and connection.

This model emphasizes the importance of space between partners, allowing attraction and passion to thrive.

The model promotes the idea of a collaborative partnership where each person contributes to something greater than themselves.

The model incorporates both masculine (goal-oriented, problem-solving) and feminine (compassion, nurturing) energies.

For Monogamy Mk2 to be effective, two key prerequisites are required: consciousness and courage. Consciousness involves awareness of personal values, beliefs, and pressures, while courage is needed to confront fears, take risks, and engage authentically in the relationship.

Conclusion

Writing this book has given me the time and space to explore my experiences with monogamy and question my expectations. In doing so, I've moved away from assumptions, allowed myself to think freely, and formed my own conclusions about relationships.

Realising that monogamy is a moral dilemma has been an enlightening journey. It's a step away from fear and a step closer to understanding the conflicts between societal norms and our natural instincts. This understanding has shed light on why past relationships often felt so tense.

Monogamy isn't a natural state; it's not something our biology is wired for. Humans, both men and women, have instincts that drive them to seek multiple partners. No amount of societal pressure can fully erase those desires. Yet, monogamy is held up as the gold standard of moral behaviour. When there's a gap between what's natural and what's considered normal, tension is bound to follow. And as long as monogamy is seen as the ultimate moral choice, those who struggle with it are often unfairly judged. In truth, they're just being human. While deceit in relationships is never okay, it's worth considering that the real surprise might be when relationships go unchallenged and commitments stay constant.

Truman Capote captured this sentiment perfectly:

"It may be normal, darling; but I'd rather be natural."

The tug-of-war between loyalty and liberty appears in many parts of our lives, but nowhere is it more evident than in our relationships. We feel the pull to stay true to tradition and community but also crave personal freedom. Even in today's world, where we have more choices than ever, there's still pressure to find a partner and settle down. It's hard to break away from the norms our parents followed, often leading us to drift into monogamy and marriage without much thought. Having a spouse is not just a personal choice but a marker of success and even self-worth. This association pushes people to choose between fitting in and exploring their own paths.

Earl Nightingale explained this succinctly:

"The opposite of courage in our society is not cowardice; it is conformity."

Because monogamy is viewed as the right and moral choice, it's risky to adopt it without reflection. As Adam Phillips says:

"If trauma is untransformable experience, then any moral belief – that is simply abided by rather than personally transformed is akin to trauma."

We should be free to ask questions, learn the truth about our nature, and experiment with different ways of connecting so that our paths are truly our own.

Through my reflections, I've come to see that while monogamy can be a source of joy, it also comes with its own set of challenges because of its inherent contradictions. There are two ways to navigate these: with openness, communication, and compassion or with judgment, blame, and conflict. The danger in continuing to see monogamy as the only moral option is that it feeds into our tendency to judge and divide based on differences. As we embrace more diverse relationship structures, like polygamy, it's important to focus on shared values, not differences. As John Stuart Mill suggested, we can find unity in the common goal of building loving and respectful relationships, whatever form they take. If we look beyond appearances and see relationships through the lens of love, we can foster a sense of community and inclusivity.

Monogamy And Maturity

One of the biggest insights I've gained is how much maturity matters in our relationship choices and dealing with our conflicting desires. By maturity, I mean not just age or experience, but a deep understanding of oneself and the ability to manage one's emotions and insecurities. Monogamy isn't a one-size-fits-all solution; it's a dynamic process shaped by the choices of the people involved. And those choices are influenced by our individual levels of insecurity and self-awareness.

Relationships are better understood as systems with inputs, processes, and outputs. The maturity each person brings into a relationship plays a huge role in how well they handle its inherent challenges. You can only love someone else as deeply as you've learned to manage your own insecurities.

Marianne Williamson beautifully captures this idea:

"We cannot give what we do not have: We cannot bring peace to the world if we are not peaceful. We cannot bring love to the world without loving ourselves. Our true gift to ourselves and others lies not in what we have but in who we are."

The maturity of each person affects many aspects of a relationship, from whether it feels like a free choice or a burden to how each defines love to how they use sex—whether as a means of connection or a tool of power.

For these reasons, it's crucial to acknowledge the complexities of monogamy and the role of self-awareness and emotional maturity in relationships. By doing so, we can empower individuals to take responsibility for their own growth and foster healthier, more harmonious relationships.

Embracing Change And Balance

Relationships are constantly evolving. The excitement of early romance naturally shifts into a more settled connection over time. Promises made at one stage in life aren't always guarantees for the future, and what feels solid today might crumble tomorrow. As Leonard Sweet said:

"Stagnation is death. If you don't change, you die. It's that simple. It's that scary."

The choice we have in navigating these changes is whether we suppress them to maintain an illusion of stability or communicate openly with our partners. The first option is sure to result in the death of the relationship.

Similarly, many people hope that being in a relationship will create an environment where both partners can thrive. But in our modern world, masculine energy—focused on progress, structure, and achievement—often dominates. It takes conscious effort to balance this with feminine energy's nurturing and restorative qualities. Feminine energy is about empathy, intuition, and emotional connection. Without this balance, relationships can feel more like hard work than a loving partnership.

Love And Understanding

One of the most valuable outcomes of this journey has been redefining what love means to me. I've explored the many forms love can take and realised that love isn't just about feelings; it's about actions—specifically, actions that reduce suffering, increase happiness, and help others reach their full potential. Emotions can fluctuate, but we always have the power to choose actions based on care and compassion. And while we can separate from another, love can still exist between the exes.

This perspective has shown me that love doesn't die—it changes form. The intense passion of Eros might give way to the steadiness of Pragma. Still, love persists when we act with openness, honesty, and integrity. I've also come to appreciate the idea from the Bible that "love rejoices with the truth." It's heartening to think that love within a monogamous relationship should be strong enough to:

- Acknowledge that monogamy isn't natural.
- Accept that desire for others is part of being human.
- Recognise that we have different mental pathways for lust, romance, and attachment.
- Embrace the evolving nature of love.
- Support open and honest conversations about individual needs and shared goals.
- Enjoy the ongoing process of understanding ourselves and our partners.

Thich Nhat Hanh teaches that love is synonymous with understanding, and understanding others begins with understanding ourselves. We can only empathise with another's struggles when we've faced our own, and we can only support another's dreams when we recognise our desires. To build authentic relationships, we need to explore:

- The complexities of human nature and how they affect coupledom.
- How natural laws align with our views on partnership.

- Our own definitions of love and the actions needed to sustain it.
- Our life goals and the role relationships play in them.
- Our level of maturity and its influence on decisions.
- How we link sex, love, and self-worth.
- How fear might cloud our judgment and hinder compassionate choices.

One of the great lessons for me has been understanding the importance of self-love in successful relationships. What I once might have dismissed as selfish, I now see as essential. For the more I care for myself, the more I can offer to others. Moreover, I can only provide honest empathy for another's darkness when I have done the same for myself.

While this book has provided many answers, it has also raised many new questions, and I am thrilled about that. Because I fundamentally believe that we grow both individually and as a society when we approach issues with curiosity and when we challenge conventions with compassion. We have all seen how much trauma the continued break up of families creates, but I know that we can do things differently if we come back to the core of what truly matters - love. I hope that this book has helped you think more about how you can construct connections where love and understanding are at the centre.

About the Author

Belinda Tobin is a researcher, author, producer, and avid explorer of the human experience, with all its challenges and complexities. Her works span fiction, non-fiction, poetry, tv series and film. However, they all share a common purpose, to foster a more conscious, compassionate and connected future.

Find out more about Belinda and her projects at www.belindatobin.com.

References

[1] Marcel, G. (2017). *The Mystery of Being*. Andesite Press.

[2] MONOGAMY Synonyms: 100 Synonyms & Antonyms for MONOGAMY | Thesaurus.com.

[3] Brunning, L. (2020). *Does Monogamy Work? A Primer for the 21st Century* (The Big Idea Series) (1st ed.). Thames & Hudson.

[4] Australian Bureau of Statistics, Religious Affiliation in Australia, 04/07/2022.

[5] The Share of Never-Married Americans Has Reached a New High. (2022). *Institute for Family Studies*. https://ifstudies.org/blog/the-share-of-never-married-americans-has-reached-a-new-high.

[6] Office for National Statistics in the UK as quoted in [3].

[7] Phillips, A. (1999). *Monogamy*. Van Haren Publishing.

[8] We've Been Designed to Reproduce | Psychology Today.

[9] William McDougall: An Introduction to Social Psychology: Chapter 10: The Reproductive and the Parental Instincts. (n.d.).

[10] Mock and Fujioka. 1990. Monogamy and long-term pair bonding in vertebrates. Trends in Ecology and Evolution 5(2): 39-43.

[11] The research of Walter Scheidel, as quoted in Brunning, L. (2020). Does Monogamy Work?: A Primer for the 21st Century (The Big Idea Series) (1st ed.). Thames & Hudson.

[12] Toyofa and Spitzberg. 2007. The dark side of infidelity: Its nature, prevalence, and communicative functions.

[13] Betzig 1989. Causes of conjugal dissolution. Current Anthropology 30:654-76.

[14] Marín, R. A., Christensen, A., & Atkins, D. C. (2014). Infidelity and behavioral couple therapy: Relationship outcomes over 5 years following therapy. Couple and Family Psychology: Research and Practice, 3(1), 1–12. https://doi.org/10.1037/cfp0000012.

[15] S. (2021, March 11). Infidelity: The Cold Hard Truth About Cheating. LA Intelligence. https://laintelligence.com/infidelity-the-cold-hard-truth-about-cheating/

[16] Fisher, H. (2017). *Anatomy of Love: A Natural History of Mating, Marriage, and Why We Stray* (Completely Revised and Updated with a New Introduction ed.). W. W. Norton & Company.

[17] Based on the discussions found in Social Basis of Human Sexual Behavior. (n.d.). https://public.wsu.edu/ per cent7Etaflinge/socsex.html

[18] *Male mixed reproductive strategies in biparental species*: American naturalist 2005.

[19] Brunning, L. (2020). *Does Monogamy Work?*: A Primer for the 21st Century (1st ed.). Thames & Hudson.

[20] Fisher, H. (2017). *Anatomy of Love: A Natural History of Mating, Marriage, and Why We Stray* (Completely Revised and Updated with a New Introduction ed.). W. W. Norton & Company.

[21]] Grinde, B. (2009). *Can the concept of discords help us find the causes of mental diseases?* Medical Hypotheses, 73(1), 106–109. https://doi.org/10.1016/j.mehy.2009.01.030

[22] Grinde, Bjørn & Patil, Grete. (2009). *Biophilia: Does Visual Contact with Nature Impact on Health and Wellbeing?* International journal of environmental research and public health. 6. 2332-43. 10.3390/ijerph6092332.

[23] Robert, B. (2020). *Sin and Sex* (Routledge Revivals) (1st ed.). Routledge.

[24] Seneca quoted in Coontz, S. (2006). *Marriage, a History: How Love Conquered Marriage*. Adfo Books.

[25] De Beauvoir, S., Borde, C., & Malovany-Chevallier, S. (2011). The Second Sex. Van Haren Publishing.

[26] Coontz, S. (2006). *Marriage, a History: How Love Conquered Marriage*. Adfo Books

[27] Note that the existence of chastity belts is now contested and viewed more as a metaphor rather than an actual genital guard.

[28] Coontz, S. (2006). *Marriage, a History: How Love Conquered Marriage*. Adfo Books

[29] The Origin of the Family, Private Property and the State (1884) by Friedrich Engles

[30] Marriages and Divorces, Australia, 2021 | Australian Bureau of Statistics (abs.gov.au)

[31] Perel, E. (2012). Mating in Captivity: How to keep desire and passion alive in long-term relationships. Hodder & Stoughton.

[32] John Stuart Mills, as quoted in Phillips, A. (2021). *On Wanting to Change*. Penguin.

[33] Mill, J., & Benitez, P. (2017). *On Liberty* John Stuart Mill. Van Haren Publishing.

[34] Gray, J. (2002). *Straw Dogs: Thoughts on Humans and Other Animals*. Granta.

[35] Barash, D. P., & Lipton, J. E. (2002). *The Myth of Monogamy: Fidelity and Infidelity in Animals and People*. Holt Paperbacks.

[36] Phillips, A. (1999). *Monogamy*. Vintage.

[37] Botton, A. D. E. (2015). *Essays In Love* (Main Market Ed.). Pan Macmillan India.

[38] These Are the 7 Types of Love | Psychology Today

[39] Dethmer, J., Chapman, D and Klemp, K., n.d. *The 15 Commitments Of Conscious Leadership*.

[40] Fisher, H. (2017). Anatomy of Love: A Natural History of Mating, Marriage, and Why We Stray (Completely Revised and Updated with a New Introduction ed.). W. W. Norton & Company.

[41] Tennov, D. (1998). *Love and Limerence: The Experience of Being in Love*. Penguin Random House.

[42] Liebowitz, M. R. (1983). The Chemistry of Love. Little, Brown.

[43] Hanh, N. T., & DeAntonis, J. (2019). At Home in the World: Stories and Essential Teachings from a Monk's Life (Reprint). Parallax Press.

[44] Greer, G. (2008). The Female Eunuch. Harper Perennial Modern Classics.

[45] Greer, G. (2008). The Female Eunuch. Harper Perennial Modern Classics.

[46] Mate, G. N., Neufeld, G., & Maté, G. (2019). Hold on to Your Kids: Why Parents Need to Matter More Than Peers. Van Haren Publishing.

[47] Kegan, R. (1983). The Evolving Self. Amsterdam University Press.

[48] Numerous references as cited in Zhang, S. (2017). *Investigating the Possible Effects of Disney Princess Culture on Young Women:* Approach, Ideals, and Gender Roles Within Intimate Relationships. Thesis for City University of Seattle.

[49] Fisher, H. (2017). *Anatomy of Love: A Natural History of Mating, Marriage, and Why We Stray* (Completely Revised and Updated with a New Introduction ed.). W. W. Norton & Company.

[50] Numerous references as cited in Zhang, S. (2017). *Investigating the Possible Effects of Disney Princess Culture on Young Women:* Approach, Ideals, and Gender Roles Within Intimate Relationships. Thesis for City University of Seattle.

[51] *god.* (2023). In The Merriam-Webster.com Dictionary. https://www.merriam-webster.com/dictionary/god

[52] Mill, J., & Benitez, P. (2017). *On Liberty* John Stuart Mill. Van Haren Publishing.

[53] IC 35-31.5-2-302

[54] Associated Press. (2022, April 24). After Utah Decriminalized Polygamy, Some See a Culture Shift. US News & World Report. https://www.usnews.com/news/best-states/utah/articles/2022-04-24/after-utah-decriminalized-polygamy-some-see-a-culture-shift

[55] "Polyamory Action Lobby". Hansard: Australian Parliament House. 28 February 2013. Retrieved 1 October 2015.

[56] Family, domestic and sexual violence data in Australia, Crime rates for family and domestic violence - Australian Institute of Health and Welfare (aihw.gov.au)

[57] AIHW, (2021): AIHW (2022): Specialist homelessness services annual report 2021–22.

[58] AIHW (2019): *Family, domestic and sexual violence in Australia: continuing the national story 2019*. Canberra: AIHW

[59] Phillips, A. (2012). *Missing Out: In Praise of the Unlived Life*. Penguin UK.

[60] Hegel 'A fragment on love' The philosophy of erotic love eds. Solomon, Rober C and Kethleen M. Higgins. University press of Kansas 1991 as cited in Cleary, S. (2022). *How to Be You: Simone de Beauvoir and the art of authentic living*. Random House.

[61] Dethmer, J., Chapman, D and Klemp, K., n.d. *The 15 Commitments Of Conscious Leadership*.

[62] As discussed in Cleary, S. (2022). How to Be You: Simone de Beauvoir and the art of authentic living. Random House.

[63] Moore, T. (1998). The Soul of Sex: Cultivating Life as an Act of Love. Harper.

[64] Perel, E. (2012c). Mating in Captivity: How to keep desire and passion alive in long-term relationships. Hachette UK.

[65] As discussed in Cleary, S. (2022). How to Be You: Simone de Beauvoir and the art of authentic living. Random House.

[66] As discussed in Moore, T. (2014). A Religion of One's Own: A Guide to Creating a Personal Spirituality in a Secular World. Penguin.

UP

UNDERSTANDING PRESS

For more titles go to:

www.heart-led.pub/understanding-press